Police Officers (

A Handbook for Police Officers of England, Scotland and Wales

1st Edition

Jeremy A Green

BA Hons

Copyright

ISBN: 978-1-4717-1123-7

Contents

Foreword

The past year as seen many changes in the police force with the Windsor report part I and II having an impact on what police officers earn and how they work. The 20% cuts have continued to bite and forces have had to look towards ways of making savings. We have even seen private security firm G4S being contracted to design, build and run a police station in Lincolnshire, in what is thought to be one of the most radical outsourcing deals seen so far in Britain. Under the £200m 10 year deal signed more than 540 civilian police staff will join the company, which will deliver a range of middle and back-office services. Some forces have finally started to recruit with a mixture of internal only or internal and external applications being taken. The police force has never seen so many changes in such a short period of time.

The riots in summer of 2011 saw how much the police are relied upon in a time of need and the importance of having a robust and professional police force, with the right number of officers. Many police officers saw the public's appreciation first hand as various Facebook pages appeared to offer support to the police during and after the riots.

Being a Police officer is still an extraordinary job done by extraordinary people. It is a job that never ends not for Public Holidays or Christmas day. The job requires a group of people who can work around the clock and work shifts. The variety of roles is huge and is a career and a job for life for many. You may start as a Constable and end up as a Chief Constable. You may move out of uniform into CID or into one of the specialist branches such as firearms, traffic, dogs or mounted; the opportunities are wide and varied.

A Police officer has a complicated job and requires numerous skills and that is what this book is aimed at doing. By going through some of the skills required and giving an insight into what being a uniformed Police officer is all about. Be it a Special Constable or full-time regular officer.

Thanks to Jayne Walters for her excellent training and support with this book. Graham Collington as well as being a good friend and colleague is always on hand for helpful advice and guidance, Kelly Warwick and Dave Wesson the best beat team you could work with and finally my Wife & family.

UK LAW ENFORCEMENT AND ITS HISTORY

Law enforcement in the United Kingdom is organised separately in each of the legal systems of the United Kingdom England, Wales, Northern Ireland, and Scotland (administration of Police matters is not generally affected by the Government of Wales Act 2006). Geographical Police areas are arranged to match the boundaries of one or more local government areas. There are four general types of body, the first mostly concerned with policing the general public and their activities and the rest concerned with policing of other, usually localised, matters. There are 43 Police forces in England and Wales formed of more than 137,500 Police officers, 17,000 volunteer Special Constables and 13,400 Community Support Officers. Scotland has 16,675 Police officers and Northern Ireland has 10,330 Police officers. Recruitment for the Special Constabluary mainly due to the riots of 2011 saw a 50% increase in the number of application requests.

Territorial Police forces, who carry out the majority of policing. These are Police forces that cover a 'Police area' (a particular region) and have an independent Police Authority. The Police Act 1996, the Police (Scotland) act 1967 and the Police (Northern Ireland) act 2000, prescribe a number of issues such as appointment of a Chief Constable, jurisdiction and responsibilities, for Police forces in England and Wales, Scotland and Northern Ireland respectively.

Special Police forces, which are national Police forces that have a specific, non-regional jurisdiction, such as the British Transport Police. The Serious Organised Crime and Police Act 2005 refers to these as 'Special Police forces'.

Non-Police law enforcement agencies, whose officers are not Police officers, but still enforce laws.

Miscellaneous forces, mostly having their foundations in older legislation or common law. These have a responsibility to Police specific local areas or activities, such as ports and parks and before the passing of recent legislation such as the Serious Organised Crime and Police Act 2005 were often referred to as 'Special Police forces'; care must therefore be taken in interpreting historical use of that phrase. These constabularies are not within the scope of the legislation applicable to the previously-mentioned organisations but can still be the subject of statutes applicable to e.g. docks, harbours or railways. Until the passing of Railways and Transport Safety act 2003, the British Transport Police was such a force.

In the United Kingdom, every person has limited powers of arrest if they see a crime being committed - these are called 'every person powers', commonly referred to as a 'citizen's arrest'. In England and Wales, the vast majority of attested constables enjoy full powers of arrest and search as granted by the Police and Criminal Evidence Act 1984. All Police officers are "constables" in law, irrespective of rank. Although Police officers have wide ranging powers, they are still civilians and subject to the same laws as members of the public. However there are certain legal restrictions on Police officers such as the illegality of taking industrial action and the ban on taking part in active politics.

Territorial Police Constables
Most police officers are members of territorial police forces. Upon taking an oath for one of these forces, they have jurisdiction in one of the three distinct legal system - either

England and Wales, Scotland or Northern Ireland. A police officer of one of the three legal systems has all the powers of a Constable throughout their own legal system but limited powers in the other two legal systems. Certain exceptions where full Police powers cross the border with the officer are when officers are providing planned support to another force such as the G8

Conference in Scotland in 2005, officers of the Metropolitan Police who are on protection duties anywhere in the United Kingdom and when taking a person to or from a prison.

Special Constabulary
The Special Constabulary is the part-time volunteer section of a statutory Police force in the United Kingdom or Crown dependency. Its officers are known as Special Constables (all hold the office of Constable no matter what their rank) or informally as Specials, SC or SPC.

Every United Kingdom territorial Police force has a Special Constabulary except the Police Service of Northern Ireland, where it is called the Reserve: however, the Royal Ulster Constabulary did have its own Ulster Special Constabulary, which was disbanded in 1970. The British Transport Police also has a Special Constabulary; in the Crown dependencies, the Isle of Man Constabulary and the States of Guernsey Police Service have Special constabularies, but the States of Jersey Police does not.

The strength of the Special Constabulary in England and Wales, as at 31 March 2008, was 14,000, and currently stands at around 17,000 with about a third of these being women and over 3% ethnic minorities. There is a push to raise this number to 20,000 through extra government funding. Special constables usually work for a minimum of four hours a week, although many do considerably more. Special constables might receive some expenses and allowances from the Police service, including a "recognition award" or "Bounty" of up to £1000 in Scotland. Some forces in England have this too but the work is otherwise voluntary and unpaid.

Special constables have identical powers to their regular (full-time) colleagues and work alongside regular Police officers. Most special Constabularies in England and Wales have their own organisational structure and grading system. For example, some use section Officers as opposed to Special Sergeants and the structure does vary from force to force. Special Constabularies are headed by a Commandant or Chief Officer, who are themselves Special Constables. Within Scotland, and a number of forces in England and Wales, plus the British Transport Police, Special Constables have no separate administrative structure and no grading system.

Special constables generally wear uniforms identical to that of their full-time colleagues. In some constabularies, their shoulder. (or collar) number may be prefixed with a certain digit or they may have additional insignia on their epaulettes. This is usually a crown with the letters SC underneath it (although some forces just use the letters). Formerly, male Special Constables did not wear helmets while on foot patrol but wore patrol caps instead, but in most forces they now wear helmets of the same design as full-time officers. Some forces also issue Special Constables with a different hat badge from that of their regular counterparts although this is now extremely rare.

Historically, Special Constables were often seen as inferior and resented by regular officers, as they were sometimes seen as "hobby bobbies" and not proper Police officers. During the 1980s Specials were often considered to be preventing regular officers from earning overtime pay. Today, Specials and regulars have a much closer relationship (many regular officers having started their Police careers as Specials) and Specials are a supplement to any Police force. Some regulars and Specials work together as a team and of course, Specials are an important part of Neighborhood Teams.

A sizeable proportion of regular officers have served as Special Constables before joining the regular force, and this is encouraged by recruitment departments. Allowing Special Constables to be paid for their work has been a contentious issue, with mixed comments from all sides. Some people think that as Specials are doing much the same job as regular officers they should be paid the same, but others think that this would attract the 'wrong' type of person (those motivated by monetary gain as opposed to those who are community minded).

This greater acceptance of Specials has led to them being found working in such areas as Public Order Units (PSU, or Police Support Unit) or Roads Policing, and some Specials have been response trained, which allows them to use blue lights and to pursue other vehicles.

Police Civilians
In England & Wales, the chief police officer of a territorial police force may designate any person who is employed by the Police authority maintaining that force, and is under the direction and control of that chief police officer, as one or more of the following:

Community support officer (commonly referred to as a police Community Support Officer), Investigating officer, Detention officer, or escort officer.

They have a range of powers given by the Police Reform act 2002, and their chief police officer decides which of these powers they may use. Unlike a police constable, a police Community Support Officer (PCSO) only has powers when on duty and in uniform, and within the area policed by their respective force.

Until 1991, most parking enforcement was carried out by Police-employed Traffic Wardens. Since the passage of the Road Traffic Act 1991, decriminalised parking enforcement has meant that most local authorities have taken on this role and now only the Metropolitan Police employs Traffic Wardens, combining the role with PCSOs as "Traffic Police Community Support Officers".

In Scotland, Police Custody and Security Officers have powers similar to those of detention officers and escort officers in England and Wales. Similar powers are available in Northern Ireland.

Accredited Persons
Chief Police officers of territorial Police forces (and the BTP) can also give limited powers to people not employed by the Police authority, under Community Safety Accreditation Schemes. A notable example is officers of the Vehicle and Operator services Agency, who have been given powers to stop vehicles. However, this practice has been criticised by the Police Federation who described it as 'half-baked'.

Members of the Armed Forces

In Northern Ireland only, members of Her Majesty's Armed Forces have powers to stop people or vehicles, arrest and detain people for three hours and enter buildings to keep the peace or search for people who have been kidnapped. Additionally, commissioned officers may close roads. They may use reasonable force when exercising these powers.

Under the Customs Management act 1979, members of Her Majesty's Armed Forces may detain people if they believe they have committed an offence under the Customs & Excise acts, and may seize goods if they believe they are liable to forfeiture under the same acts.

Other Civilians

Many employees of local authorities have powers of entry relating to inspection of businesses, such as under the Sunday Trading act 1994 and powers to give Fixed Penalty Notices for offences such as littering, graffiti or one of the wide ranging offences in the Clean Neighborhoods and Environment act 2005. Further such powers may be given under local bylaws or local acts of Parliament. These are often street wardens or dog wardens.

When carrying out an investigation, staff of the Independent Police Complaints Commission has all the powers and privileges of constables throughout England and Wales and the territorial waters.

Employees of the Serious Organised Crime Agency can be designated with the powers of a Constable, Revenue and Customs officer and immigration officer. These designations can be unconditional or conditional: time limited or limited to a specific operation.

Employees of the UK Border Agency may be Immigration Officers and/or customs officers. They hold certain powers of arrest, detention and search.

In England & Wales, water bailiffs employed by the Environment Agency have certain powers in relation to enforcement of fishing regulations. Scottish water bailiffs have similar powers. There are also seven types of court officer - two in Scotland and five in England & Wales, commonly referred to as 'bailiffs', who can enforce court orders and in some cases arrest people.

Traffic officers are employed by the Highways Agency and maintain traffic flows on trunk roads and some bridges and tunnels. There are different types of traffic officer, and they are appointed under separate acts. They have limited powers to direct traffic and place road signs.

Wildlife inspectors have certain powers of entry and inspection in relation to wildlife and licenses relating to wildlife.

Employees of public fire and rescue services have extensive powers in the event of an emergency, and more limited ones in certain other circumstances, such as investigations into fires.

Prison officers have all the powers, authority, protection and privileges of a Constable when acting as prison officers.

Other Constables
There are many constables who are not members of territorial Police forces. The most notable are members of the three forces referred to as 'Special Police forces': the British Transport Police, Ministry of Defence Police and Civil Nuclear

Constabulary. These officers have the 'powers and privileges of a Constable' on land relating to their work and in matters relating to their work. BTP (British Transport Police) and MDP officers have additional jurisdiction where requested by a Constable of another force, in which case they take on that constables jurisdiction. Upon request from the chief Police officer of a Police force, members of one of the above three forces can be give the full powers of constables in the Police area of the requesting force. This was used to supplement Police numbers in the areas surrounding the 2005 G8 summit at Gleneagles.

There are also many acts which allow companies or councils to employ constables for a specific purpose. Firstly, there are ten companies whose employees are sworn in as constables under section 79 of the Harbours, Docks, and Piers Clauses act 1847. As a result, they have the full powers of a Constable on any land owned by the harbour, dock, or port and at any place within one mile of any owned land. Secondly, there are also some forces created by specific legislation such as the Port of Tilbury Police (Port of London act 1968), Mersey Tunnels Police (County of Merseyside act 1989) and the Epping Forest Keepers (Epping Forest act 1878).

Thirdly, under Article 18 of the Ministry of Housing and Local Government Provisional Order Confirmation (Greater London Parks and Open Spaces) act 1967, London Borough Councils are allowed to swear in council officers as constables for "securing the observance of the provisions of all enactments relating to open spaces under their control or management and of bye-laws and regulations made thereunder". These constables are not legally Police Constables and have no powers to enforce criminal law other than those afforded to every citizen.

History of UK Police

There have always been criminals but we did not always have cops.

The first steps in policing the country came in 1361 with the Justice of the Peace Act. In each county, three or four men were appointed to 'arrest, take and chastise' offenders.

The industrial revolution caused a huge influx of people from the country to cities. With it came poverty, which caused a law and order crisis. Into this chaos came Henry Fielding, who formed the first paid Police force, known as The Runners.

The Bow Street Runners were a small, plain-clothed force that started in 1750. They sought help from the public by publishing descriptions of criminals. By 1805, The Runners were joined by the Bow Street Horse Patrol, who helped to clear London of highwaymen. Similar to the unofficial 'thief-takers' (men who would solve petty crime for a fee), they represented a formalisation and regularisation of existing policing methods. What made them different from the thief-takers was their formal attachment to the Bow Street magistrates' office, and that they were paid by the magistrate with funds from central government. They worked out of Fielding's office and court at No. 4 Bow Street, and did not patrol but served writs and arrested offenders on the authority of the magistrates, travelling nationwide to apprehend criminals.

When Henry Fielding retired as 'court' or Chief magistrate in 1754 he was succeeded by his brother John Fielding, who had previously been his assistant for four years. Known as the "Blind Beak of Bow Street", John Fielding refined the patrol into the first truly effective Police force for the capital, later adding officers mounted on horseback.

Although the force was only funded intermittently in the years that followed, it did serve as the guiding principle for the way policing was to develop over the next 80 years: Bow Street was a manifestation of the move towards increasing professionalisation and state control of street life, beginning in London.

Contrary to several popular sources, the Bow Street Runners were not nicknamed "Robin Redbreasts", this epithet being reserved for the Bow Street Horse Patrol. The Horse Patrol, organised in 1805 by Sir John Fielding's successor at Bow Street, Richard Ford, wore a distinctive scarlet waistcoat under their blue greatcoats.

Peelers and Bobbies In 1822 Sir Robert Peel entered the Cabinet as home secretary in the government of Lord Liverpool. He distinguished himself in this post through a series of penal reforms, including the reform of criminal laws and the reduction of the number of crimes that carried the death penalty. In 1829, convinced of the need for improved methods of crime prevention, Peel reorganized the Bow Street Runners into the London Metropolitan Police force, thereafter called "bobbies", after his first name.

With the Metropolitan Police Bill of 1829. He approved a force of 95 constables, 88 sergeants and 20 inspectors. By 1856, over 200 Police forces were established in England and Wales. These were the true forerunners of modern policing, as we know it.

Uniformed truncheons people hated the new Police so much that uniforms were designed to make them look like civilians. Wearing dark blue coats and a collar with their Constable's number hence the name collar number still used today. They carried truncheons and a rattle to raise the alarm. By 1864, helmets were introduced and whistles replaced rattles.

History of the Special Constabulary

The history of the Special Constable is a long and honourable one. From time immemorial, ordinary citizens have been called upon to assist the regular forces of law and order.

Traditionally, in the days before Robert Peel introduced professional policing, the Constable of a town or village swore in fellow citizens when a situation arose that he alone could not handle, such as on market days or in times of public unrest.

While the idea of the citizens or populous policing itself dates back to Anglo-Saxon times (with English common law requiring that all citizens have the legal obligation to come to the assistance of a Police officer) it was not until 1673, when Charles II ruled that citizens could be temporarily sworn in as constables during times of public disorder. This ruling was in response to rising public disorder relating to the enforcement of religious conformity, and any citizen refusing to acknowledge the call would have been subject to fines and jail sentences. The 1673 act was enforced for centuries after, but mainly used to call up constables in the north of England.

Public disorder of that nature was renewed during the industrial revolution in the 18th and 19th centuries, which was coupled with falling living standards and starvation. In 1819, mass meetings calling for Parliamentary reform took place across

England, including 60,000 demonstrators rioting in Manchester, where a Special Constable was killed. In light of these events, in 1820, an Act was passed allowing magistrates to recruit men as Special Constables.

The earliest legislation relating to Specials was the Special Constables Act of 1831. This officially gave the chief Police officer of a district the power to appoint Special Constables on a temporary basis as a result of specific occurrences. This meant that in the 1840s during the time of the protest marches and demonstrations of the political reformers known as the Chartists, many thousands of specials were enrolled.

During the First World War, the national emergency and the recall of many regular Police officers to their regiments led Chief Constables to enrol many specials. The Special Constables Act 1914 was passed, allowing the Chief Constable to appoint Specials even though "a tumult, riot or felony had not taken place". The outcome of this act was to establish Specials as a permanent feature throughout the war, as opposed to being the temporary force of earlier years. An Inspector of the regular Police was in charge of each district. The superintendent of each of the regular Police Divisions was in overall command of the Specials on the division.

In addition to foot patrols, specials also carried out a number of mounted patrols, with the officers acting as traffic police. Where possible a full uniform with peaked cap was provided and for off duty wear an enamelled lapel badge for civilian clothing was authorised. Many men also wore a badge inscribed "On War Duty". Normally these were issued to persons with reserved occupations. The badge could prevent the presentation of a white feather for cowardice by those misguided members of the public swept away in the patriotic fervour of the early war years.

After the war, decorated truncheons were presented to all Specials, bearing the name of the individual and the coat of arms of the city or borough that he had served. In the 1920s, the Specials were largely disbanded, although the value of their service was not forgotten and the provisions of the 1914 act were reinforced by the 1923 Special Constables Act. This confirmed the permanent nature of the specials and allowed for the employment of them in naval, military and air force yards and stations. It also removed some restrictions on the appointment of Specials in Scotland. Also laid down at this time were regulations regarding the reimbursement of out-of-pocket expenses. However, Specials were enrolled again a few years later during the General Strike of 1926. While civilian volunteers manned buses and the army provided escorts for food lorries and other supplies, many thousands of Specials were required to help maintain vital services. Many volunteers received no uniform, merely an armband, and after the event decorated truncheons were presented by some towns and cities to those who had served. The next great test came during the Second World War when again the call for volunteers was answered, often by men too old for the armed services, but willing to help out on the home front. They topped up police forces depleted by the return of men to the services and stretched by extra duties such as civil defence, air raid precautions and the supervision of foreign nationals - friendly or otherwise.

After the war, the specials remained as a permanent complement to police forces and have remained so until today. At present Special Constables attend a basic recruit training course at a training school. The training includes criminal law, first aid and traffic regulations. Some forces undertake mock court hearings and staged accidents to help to liven up training and boost the Specials' confidence. After training they are posted to Divisions under the guide of a tutor, and are usually required to complete a professional development portfolio. Tours of duty are normally four hours a week as a minimum and, while unpaid, allowances are available and out-of-pocket expenses are reimbursed. Their uniforms and equipment are the same as those used by the regulars. With the decrease in full-time officer numbers Special Constables are in even greater demand with most forces looking to double the number of specials they have.

Police Vehicles
In 1858, the first police vehicle was horse drawn, later secure Police vehicles were introduced. They were called originally Black Marias; a special area in the yard of Bow Street Police court was reserved for the loading and unloading of Marias. From horse drawn the Police moved towards motor vehicles the first was used by the Flying Squad. This was a 1927 Lea Francis with the registration A 209, the registration is still in use today. This car was followed in by 1933 by a Fordson Van. Since then the Police have had a variety of vehicles from Jaguar, Woolsey, Austin, Daimler, Ford, Mini, to name a few including the iconic Ford Zephyr and Rover SD1.

Today it is a mixture of Volvo V70 T5/D5, BMW 3 and 5 Series, Vauxhall Astra and Vectra, Ford Focus and Mondeo these being the more common cars used by the various police forces. But you may also see Subaru Impreza, Mitsubishi Evo, Range Rover, Land Rover Discovery, Jaguar XF and Skoda Octavia VRS. Along with cars some Police forces have a variety of motorbikes and van's some forces have lorries as well. In

2010 the government started a list of preferred suppliers Ford being the first on the list followed by Vauxhall, Hyundai, Jaguar, and Peugeot along with some Audi, BMW and Mitsubishi cars.

Policewomen

It wasn't until 1914 that women joined the police ranks when men were away fighting in World War I. In 1915, Edith Smith was sworn in as the first Policewoman with powers of arrest. Initially women were known as WPC (Women Police Constable) and later the W was dropped so that regardless of gender all Police officers are now known as PC (Police Constable).

The modern police service is a varied, multi-layered, responsive institution working to ensure the safety of the public.

The police force is changing. These days it is not just made up of officers and staff, but is augmented by volunteer Special Constables and highly focused Community Support Officers. All three branches walk beats, work closely with the public, and fight crime in their own ways. Forces are working together more closely to share resources and reduce costs. The future may see forces join together to form "Regional" forces or the "Super" force. With the recent 20% cuts the police service has never had such tight budgets and difficult decisions have had to be made. These have resulted in compulsory redundancies under the "A19" banner. After two years many forces now need to recruit as the numbers drop below a level that is tenable.

Special Constable's and PCSO's have become an even more important resource supporting the full-time police officers and dealing with low level crime to release full-time officers to deal with more serious incidents.

BECOMING A POLICE OFFICER

So you want to become a police officer? How do you go about it? What does it mean?

The best place to start is what you will be expected to do and what you might find you will do being as a police officer.

A Police officer is a warranted employee of a police force. Police officers are generally responsible for apprehending criminals, maintaining public order, and preventing and detecting crimes. Police officers are sworn to an oath, and are granted the power to arrest and imprison suspects, along with other practices.

You can either decide to join as a full-time police officer or become a volunteer officer known as a Special Constable.

Special Constabulary Role

The Special Constabulary forms part of the neighborhood policing teams, working alongside regular police officers, PCSOs and their partners. The primary role of the Special Constabulary is specifically to provide a high visibility presence (therefore reducing the fear of crime), dealing with anti-social behaviour and gathering and acting upon community intelligence.

As a Special Constable you will be part of the neighborhood team, as part of a larger government initiative. Some Specials do all of their time with these teams whilst some do a proportion of their time with them and the rest being spent with what is known as Response or Reactive. These are the police officers who respond to 999 calls from the public which can be anything from a Road Traffic Collision (RTC) to a fight at a local pub or a theft from a shop.

Any constabulary will ensure that you are fully trained to deal with policing problems that are affecting local communities. As a Special Constable you hold the same powers as a full-time officer – powers throughout the whole of England and Wales.

How to Become a Special Constable

To be eligible you must meet the following basic criteria:

You must be a national of a country within the European Economic Area or, if a national of a country outside the EEA, have the right to reside in this country without restrictions.

You must be 18 years of age or over.

You cannot be working in an occupation that would conflict with your duties as a Special Constable. Some of these occupations include: Traffic Warden, Security, Licencee, private detective, and magistrate. Anything that may bring you into conflict with your role as a Police officer is worth checking. Contact your local force for their list if you feel you current job may be an issue.

If you meet the criteria you can either contact the local force directly, or speak to the Specials recruitment officer. Many constabularies have downloadable application forms and information on their website. You can simply fill out the form, print and post or email it to the recruitment section of the force you are applying to.

As a special, most forces will expect you to be willing to undertake duty time to the equivalent of a minimum of four hours per week, which is the standard minimum. You must be willing to undertake an initial training course and attend regular training at your chosen division or station, in order to maintain your skills.

As a serving Special Constable you will personally benefit from:

New experiences – you can expect to enjoy much of the variety that comes along with police work.

New people – you will be working as one of a team and the experiences you share in working closely together can lead to lasting friendships. You will learn more about life and human nature than most people will ever see.

New skills – you will learn new skills and develop existing ones, such as problem solving, negotiating, decision-making, coping with pressure, communications and inter-personal skills. These skills will help you not only as a Special, but also in your daily life, as well as in your current workplace. This will be supported by the force's appraisal system.

Most forces will pay your travelling expenses from home/work to your Police station and also offer a boot allowance of £50-70 or more. Some forces are now running bounty schemes for the completion of set hours or objectives. An example is a £500 tax deductible bounty for doing 300 or more duty hours in a year.

How to Become a Full-time Regular Officer
Full-time officers do pretty much the same roles and duties as Special Constables although being full time they often deal with much more serious crime. The options open to them during their career are wider and more varied. All police officers start as Police Constables regardless of age and experience. Then after their probationary period they can apply to join the very varied

Traffic Police, Armed response or a Beat Manager are open to those that want to stay in uniform you may want to become a detective and move into CID. Other highly sought after roles such as dog handler, mounted or air support.

Some police officers may be trained in special duties such as; counter-terrorism, surveillance, child protection, VIP protection, and investigation techniques into major crime, such as fraud, rape, murder or drug trafficking.

Police Constables Pay as of June 2012

On commencing Service	£23,259
On completion of training	£25,962
2	£27,471 (a)
3	£29,148
4	£30,066
5	£31,032
6	£31,917
7	£32,703
8	£33,753
9	£35,796
10	£36,519

a) All officers move to this salary point on completion of two years' service as a constable.

Alongside the main pay scale under the Windsor review was the addition of an unsocial hour's bonus that will be paid pro rata for the hours worked between 8pm and 6am. For a constable this is up to £1200 for a constable working a standard eight-hour alternating shift pattern.

Shift Pattern
Being a police officer is a 24 hour 7 days a week 365 days a year job. That is broken down into shift work an example of a typical set of shifts might be:
2 days 7 till 4pm

2 days 3 till 12am

2 days 10pm till 7am

Followed by 4 days off.

As can be seen you work at all hours of the day and night at weekends, even Christmas day. The shifts can be difficult to get used to and your first night shift can feel like the longest night ever.

Beat Managers or constable working within the NPT teams may work slightly different hours some working till just 12-1am and doing two weekends out of every four.

A local police force will deal with emergencies and non-emergencies within certain agreed times and if you've been a victim of crime, they will agree with you how often and for how long you will be kept informed of progress on your case.

All Police forces across the whole of the England and Wales have signed up to provide the same level of service to their communities. This means that it will be easier for the public to have their say on how they police the local area, and guarantees that wherever they live, they can expect the same, high level of service.

Wherever anybody lives, they can get the following information by searching for their neighborhood policing team on their force website:

Contact details of the Neighborhood Policing Team

Details of the next Neighborhood Policing meeting

The neighborhood priorities

Action being taken by the police and follow-up to problems raised by the community

Local crime statistics, information and crime maps

How to get involved and help make your community safer

Neighborhood Policing

What is it? Neighborhood Policing is a style of policing that provides communities with a visible, familiar, and accessible policing team who work in partnership with other agencies, such as Council Street Wardens, licensing, local/parish council to reduce crime and anti-social behaviour and address local community safety priorities. All forces are committed to neighborhood policing within their respective areas.

As such, teams are made up of regular police officers, PCSOs who work on the front-line alongside Special Constables, and Beat Managers. PCSO's provide a visible and reassuring presence on the streets and tackling the menace of anti-social behaviour. PCSOs have different roles in different forces, but they usually patrol a beat and interact with the public, while also offering assistance to police officers at crime scenes and major events.

Depending on where they work, they could: deal with minor offences offer early intervention to deter people from committing offences provide support for front-line policing conduct house-to-house enquiries guard crime scenes provide crime prevention advice.

Although PCSOs do not have the same powers as regular police officers, they still carry a lot of responsibility, and are a crucial part of the police force. Along with Special Constables they have been established to work with their partners to ensure the right people, the right numbers and with the right skills, are in the right place at the right time. The size of each team depends on the local community needs. Members of the team concentrate on resolving local problems, such as disruptive families, drug misuse and anti-social behaviour.

One of the keys to effective neighborhood policing is active engagement, consultation and communication with local people to ensure their interests and concerns are reflected in the delivery of policing, community safety and neighborhood services. Local meetings or "Beat Surgeries" are organised so locals can have a voice.

Due to the unpredictable nature of law enforcement, police officers can encounter many dangerous situations in the course of their career. Officers face an increased risk of infectious diseases, physical injury or in some cases, death, as well as the potential for emotional disorder due to both the high stress and inherently adversarial nature of police work. These dangers are encountered in many different situations, such as the investigation, pursuit, and apprehension of criminals, motor vehicle stops, crimes, response to terrorism, and intervention in domestic disputes, investigating traffic accidents, and directing traffic. The constant risk, uncertainty and tension inherent in law enforcement and the exposure to vast amounts of human suffering and violence can lead susceptible individuals to anxiety, depression, and alcoholism.

Individuals' are drawn to police work for many reasons. Among these often include a desire to protect the public and social order from criminals and danger; a desire to hold a position of respect and authority; a disdain for or antipathy towards criminals and rule breakers; the professional challenges of the work; the employment benefits that are provided with civil service jobs in many countries; the sense of camaraderie that often holds among police; or a family tradition of police work or civil service. An important task of the recruitment activity of police agencies in many countries is screening potential candidates to determine the fitness of their character and personality for the work, often through background investigations and consultation with a psychologist. Even though Police work is very dangerous, police officers are still seen by most people as necessity to maintain order. But there are also those that dislike the police Force and what it stands for. Becoming a police officer may mean losing friends as well as gaining new ones.

Recruitment Process

The recruitment process can take several months and is very similar for both Full-time officers and Special Constables but varies from force to force. Specials do not usually have such a rigorous application form and do not attend the assessment day. Their assessment is usually done at a weekend or weekday evening. Specials requirement is not quite as standadised as regular officer recruitment and does vary between forces. However the process always includes elements from the regular recruitment assessment day, such as structured interview, IQ test/PIRT and written exercises. Your force will send you a recruitment pack outlining what their recruitment consists of and then you can refer to those specific elements in this chapter.

A typical application process for full-time officers is laid out below. Anything after the application phase can vary between different forces.

> Initial Application.
> Assessment day.
> Security vetting of yourself, your immediate family, and any other adults who may live at your address.
> Fitness Test.
> An interview.
> A full medical.

Of those that apply, only 15% are successful at becoming a Police officer and many have had to apply several times to get in.

The application form in itself is very important 60% of applicants for the role of police officer and PCSO are rejected at the application form stage. You are marked and graded on your answers to the competency questions and getting these right is a key element of your application form. The questions ask you to give examples that meet with the seven core competencies and we will cover these later. Also your eligibility requirements will be checked before your application can go to the next stage. You can even fail on using blue instead of black ink, not following the guidelines properly and even incorrect spelling, as all these things relate back to the seven core competencies that you will cover later.

Eligibility Requirements

Eligibility requirements for the police are fairly detailed listed is the main criterion that needs to be met.

Age requirements Applications can be accepted at the age of 18. There's no upper age limit for applying to the Police service, but bear in mind that the normal retirement age is 60 years and that new recruits are required to undertake a two-year probationary period.

Nationality requirements you must be a British citizen, an EC/EEA national or a Commonwealth citizen or foreign national with no restrictions on your stay in the United Kingdom.

Foreign nationals and UK citizens who have lived abroad may have to wait some time for security and vetting clearance. All applicants have to be vetted to the same standard before appointment.

Criminal record - A number of crimes will mean a definite or likely rejection of your application, including anyone who has received a formal caution in the last five years, committed a violent crime or public order offence.

Tattoos you should not have tattoos which could cause offence. Tattoos are not acceptable if they are particularly prominent, garish, offensive or undermine the dignity and authority of your role.

Financial status applicants will have their financial status checked. These checks are carried out because police officers have access to privileged information, which may make them vulnerable to corruption. Applicants with outstanding County court judgments, who have been registered bankrupt with outstanding debts, will be rejected. If you have discharged bankruptcy debts then you will need to provide a Certificate of Satisfaction with your application.

Physical fitness to ensure you are fit enough for the role, you will undertake a fitness test. There are two elements to the test and you must pass both before you can be appointed. They are looking for no more than the minimum standard needed to enable you to work effectively as a police officer. You will be given help to improve your fitness and if you prepare yourself properly, there is no reason for you to fail.

There are two elements to the test: dynamic strength and endurance fitness, and health.

Police officers encounter stressful situations, trauma, physical confrontation and work long hours on shifts. They need to be resilient enough to cope with the demands and pressures of

Police work. Applicants must therefore be in good health mentally and physically to undertake Police duties.

You will undergo a medical examination to ensure you meet the health standards required.

Eyesight applicants will have their eyesight tested at the medical assessment stage. You may be asked to go to an optician to have your eyes tested and the eyesight form filled in. Failure to pass this test will lead to rejection.

Previous applications you can only apply to one force at any one time. If you have previously applied to join the Police service and been unsuccessful, you must wait six months from your initial rejection before you can apply again.

Applicants from all backgrounds and ethnic groups are encouraged to apply. Applicants are not limited to any particular age group in fact; those who are looking for a career change are encouraged to join with valuable life experience. The minimum age to apply is 18, and there is no upper age limit, though you should bear in mind that the normal retirement age for Police Constables and sergeants is 60 at this present time but in line with many other sectors will most likely rise. You should also be aware that all new recruits, whatever their age, are required to undertake a two-year probationary period before you can look towards any career advancement.

Get Fit Before You Apply
One of the most rigorous elements of our screening process is the physical fitness training. Police Officers must be able to move quickly while carrying a lot of heavy equipment, they have to be in pretty good shape.

If you pass the assessment process, you will then have to take a physical fitness test. To pass, you will need to be reasonably fit, and able to run short distances fairly quickly. The bleep test is the most common test along with a grip test for the fitness element. Later you will also have to pass a medical examination.

Core Competencies

These are the competencies being looked at within your application, at the assessment centre and may come up in your interview. You need to try and give examples of when and where you have dealt with each of them. You are graded on your responses. Try to think of good examples that illustrate each competence. Try not to waffle and just show exactly where you have come across each competency in your day to day life. They don't have to be that current either. The aim is to look at your life experience and how you have reacted to each of the competencies. If you have experience of being a Special Constable or a PCSO these will often help you give good examples that you have experienced on duty. Many regular officers will be more than happy to offer advice and guidance by already be part of the police family. Another worthwhile point that is essential to the police force is political correctness and making sure you use the correct terminology and words that are not in any way sexist, racist or homophobic. Diversity is the key here.

Definition of Diversity

The concept of diversity encompasses acceptance and respect. It means understanding that each individual is unique, and recognizing our individual differences. These can be along the dimensions of race, ethnicity, gender, sexual orientation, socio-economic status, age, physical abilities, religious beliefs, political

beliefs, or other ideologies. It is the exploration of these differences in a safe, positive, and nurturing environment.
It is about understanding each other and moving beyond simple tolerance to embracing and celebrating the rich dimensions of diversity contained within each individual.

1. Respect for race and diversity

Considers and shows respect for the opinions, circumstances and feelings of colleagues and members of the public no matter what their race, religion, position, background, circumstances, status or appearance.

2. Team working

Develops strong working relationships inside and outside the team to achieve common goals. Breaks down barriers between groups and involves others in discussions and decisions.

3. Community and Customer Focus

Focuses on the customer and provides a high-quality service that is tailored to meet their individual needs. Understands the communities that are served and shows an active commitment to policing that reflects their needs and concerns.

4. Effective Communication

Communicates ideas and information effectively, both verbally and in writing. Uses language and a style of communication that is appropriate to the situation and people being addressed. Makes sure that others understand what is going on.

5. Problem Solving

Gathers information from a range of sources. Analyses information to identify problems and issues, and makes effective decisions.

6. Personal Responsibility

Takes personal responsibility for making things happen and achieving results. Displays motivation, commitment, perseverance and conscientiousness. Acts with a high degree of integrity.

7. Resilience

Shows resilience, even in difficult circumstances. Prepared to make difficult decisions and has the confidence to see them through.

Application Form: Competency Assessment

The four questions normally asked on the application form which are scored and graded are:

Q1 - It is vitally important that police officers show respect for others, irrespective of their background.

Try to recall an occasion when you have challenged someone's behaviour that was bullying, discriminatory or insensitive. Do not use an example where the other person was simply angry or upset. Their behaviour must have been bullying, discriminatory or insensitive. You will be assessed in this question on how positively you acted, and on how well you understood what had happened.

Examples

Someone queue jumping in the doctor's surgery or at a theme park.

A man and woman having a loud argument in a pub or nightclub.

Your child's teacher upsetting him or her at school through shouting at them.

A colleague is overheard making a hurtful remark about another worker's girlfriend

Q2 - Police officers often work in teams and it is important that you are able to work well with others, and are willing to share in the less attractive jobs.

Think of an occasion when it was necessary to work with others to get something done and where you played your part in getting a result. You will be assessed in this question on how well you co-operated with others in completing the task in hand.

Examples
The time you helped some friends move into their new flat.
Cleaning and renovating the Scout hut.

Putting together a large order at work in time to meet a deadline.

Clearing an overgrown garden.

Q3 - Police officers often need to remain calm and act logically and decisively in very difficult circumstances.

Recall an occasion when you have been in a very challenging or difficult situation and had to make a decision that perhaps others disagreed with. You will be assessed in this question on how positively you reacted in the face of difficulty and challenge.

Examples
Coming across a road accident where someone was hurt
Facing up to out of control personal debt.

Dealing with a drunken relative at a family party

Q4 - Police officers have to be able to communicate with a wide range of people, both verbally and in writing.

Try to remember an occasion when you have had to tell a person or a group something that they might have found upsetting or difficult to hear or read. You are being assessed in this question on how you deliver the message and the things you took into account when deciding how to do this.

Examples
Giving someone the sack.

Cancelling your firm's Christmas party to save money.

Informing a family member of the death of a relative.

The key to success in this part of the form is to understand the purpose of the questions, and to spend some time finding the best example in your life experiences to illustrate the point required. Many applicants simply write down a very brief and superficial experience, with no depth not bringing in key words or phrases. These lead to a low score and the application being rejected. 75% of applicants fail at the application stage due to poor examples and not answering the questions properly. It is essential that the answer is as thorough as possible. As a simple guide, look at each question and consider the following.

Firstly, try to identify what skills areas that recruiters are looking for by reading the question thoroughly.

Having done this, outline briefly what the issue or the circumstances of the event were.

State what actions you carried out to address the issue.

Stay what effect this had on the group or others.

Describe the result.

Describe how there was a positive outcome, in that the issue was solved and all parties had a positive learning experience from it.

Do not use an experience from when you were a child, and do not specifically name people.

Your examples must be specific. Don't generalise.

Core words or phrases to include in the answers include the following. "I identified", "I realised" and, "having spoken to him, I discovered that", "having identified the issue, I realised that one of my options was to...", "I decided", and so on. Notice that these are all "I" phrases and all of them demonstrate a sense of purpose and focus. The answer's need to be based around your response and your feelings, which are detailed and cover all the main points.

Remember that your answers will be graded, and that some forces may question you on the examples provided later on in the recruitment process. In addition, remember whilst everyone exaggerates slightly their involvement in certain incidents, if forces discover you are blatantly lying, they will have serious doubts about your personal integrity and any chance of recruitment will be lost.

Assessment Day
One of most harrowing phase for any prospective applicant is the assessment day. The day may consist of a competency-based structured interview, which is made up of four questions.

A numerical reasoning test.

A verbal logical reasoning test.

Two written exercises.

Four 10 minute interactive exercises.

In the interactive and written exercises, you may play the part of a newly appointed customer-services officer at a retail and leisure complex called The Westshire Centre. The Westshire Centre is a made up place created for the assessment centre only. There are other scenarios too. But most are looking at how you deal with various situations in particular diversity issues and effective communication skills. But the scenarios will also bring in resilience, customer service skills, problem solving and maybe team working. Many fall down on diversity with 30% failing the assessment centre on diversity. It is all too easy to full into simple traps such as assuming the gender of the complainant or another person.

The four interactive exercises are based around putting you into situations with actors to see how you react. You have five minutes to review the scenario and set out a plan and a further five minutes to deal with the scenario with an actor who is either an ex-police officer or civilian staff but not a professional actor.

Any scenario will have been tried and tested lots of times before you undertake it so you will be able to resolve the issues in the five minutes you have. The scenario may be dealing with an underperforming member of staff. A complaint from the member of the public about the facilities or another member of staff. The key points to being successful I will outline below after I have talked about planning. You will be provided with essential information in the form of memo/email/letter of complaint and they will give you a big hint on what the scenario will be about to aid in the planning.

So many applicants forget or do not plan what they are going to do in the scenario and under the pressure of the moment become flustered and loose valuable marks by missing out key points or elements. Planning is essential and the easiest method I have seen to plan is to use the CAR method.

Circumstances – What important/key details have you been given, look for anything that is diversity and you need to challenge. Any challenges need to be polite and explain why you think what they have said or written is unacceptable.

Action – What are you going to do, maybe list questions you will ask, what you need to say or address.

Results – What are you going to do to resolve the situation, maybe list a few options or action points for each element?

The best way to structure CAR is on the plain sheet of paper you will be provided with, spilt it up into three parts, then put the CAR headings in each section and then work through each section in the five minutes you have.

Some key points for the role playing element

The information you need in the preparation phases of the exercises will be supplied and as part of your assessment day invitation, you will be given a detailed overview of the scenario as part of the information pack. It is important to read and understand all the information fully. The interactive exercises will have you dealing with various situations based on the seven core competencies and you are then graded on how you resolve and react to each situation. Actors in the scenario play various customers and leisure centre employees.

Remember you are a customer service advisor and behave as one, never try to approach the scenarios as a police officer.

Never assume a name you have been given is male or female.

Challenge any diversity issues either said or written in a polite manner explaining why.

Odd scenarios start with an angry customer, stay calm they will have been told to only be angry for a set time. Stay calm be polite, ask them to sit down and explain the issue in a rational way.

You are watched and observed to see how you behave and interact even with other candidates. Expect the unexpected and be aware at all times during the day.

Remember the assessors are looking for you to solve the problem.

Make sure you question and probe to get all the information. If an employee maybe look at welfare issues, if a customer find out why that have that particular opinion. You will need to ask questions to get the information needed to give a resolution.

Don't make any assumptions; an underperforming member of staff for example may have reasons such as problems at home. A customer may have been given the wrong information.

You will need to make a decision on what to do; the actor will not make the decision for you. The assessors are looking at you to be decisive as part of the core competencies.

Try to keep to a timing schedule of one minute for the initial introduction to the problem, two-three minutes discussing the problem and questioning. Finally the last minute discussing your solution to the problem.

Each role play will seem to go very quick and will feel quite draining, have a plan, understand the core competencies, ensure no diversity opportunities are missed. Then your chances of getting the marks needed to pass the day will be greatly improved.

Assessment Day Structured Interview
The assessment day interview will last for up to 20 minutes and you will be asked four questions about how you have dealt with specific situations in the past. These questions will be related to the seven key competencies. You will be given up to five minutes to answer each question. The person interviewing you will stop you if you go over the five minutes. As the person interviewing you asks you the question, they will also give you a copy of the question to refer to. They may ask you further

questions to help you to give a full response. When you consider your responses to the interview questions only choose examples that you feel comfortable discussing with the person interviewing you.

Written Exercises

The written exercises are very much like the 10 minute role play exercises in that you have to read through information and then deliver a solution. In the case of the written exercises it is in the form of a letter as opposed to an actor. The written exercises are pass or fail. For the written exercise you have 20 minutes to plan and then write a response in the form of a letter. Just like the role play exercises use the CAR method and spend only five minutes on the planning, leaving 15 minutes to write a neat and error free letter. You will be graded on punctuation, spelling and grammar. Write neatly and at a pass that enables the least amount of mistakes but still convey all the information you need to get across. If you come across a word you cannot spell then think of another. Again make sure any diversity issues are addressed in your response and a solution that is both workable and creative is put in place.

As well as the ability to communicate in writing you are being assessed on your ability to understand and summarise information, see both sides of the problem, make a decision, generate creative solutions, evaluate solutions and finally convey that solution with a rationale.

Common scenarios are a parking issue at a school or nursery and a comment is made about silly blonde drivers, another is a kitchen that has failed a health inspection, complaints about lack of diversity and issues surrounding diversity within a company. All follow the same theme of raising issues that you need to come up with a solution for and more often than not some diversity comment that needs to be challenged in your letter.

PIRT/IQ Test

The other part is the Police Initial Recruitment test (PIRT) although this has been replaced at assessment centre's by two test papers but they follow similar lines and exercises to the (PIRT) and the examples given below will help for both types of testing. We will work through some examples to give you an idea of what is expected. One of the best tips is not to try and complete all the answers but to choose answers that you can give quickly and under pressure. If you find any difficulties then move onto the next question. Then re-visit any you have failed to complete. The tests are undertaken as part of an assessment day. Some forces still use PIRT for Special Constables entrance tests.

The PIRT test consists of several skills areas.

Verbal Usage Test – the ability to spell words and construct sentences accurately.

Checking Information – the ability to check information quickly and correctly.

Working with Numbers – the ability to solve numerical problems accurately.

Verbal Reasoning – the ability to reason logically when given facts about events.

The new tests being used by some forces consist of a numerical reasoning test which will ask you to answer multiple-choice questions which will measure your ability to solve number problems accurately. Also a verbal logical reasoning test were you will asked to answer multiple-choice questions which will measure your ability to make logical sense of a situation when you are given facts about it.

Example Tests

Verbal Usage Test

1. One hundred officers _____ allocated for _____ control.

A - was / croud

B - was / crowd

C - were / croud

D - were / crowd

E - none of these

2. It is _____ to bring your uniform to the training _____.

A - necesary / centre

B - necessary / centre

C - necessary / center

D - necessery / centre

E - none of these

Answers Verbal Reasoning

1=D

2=B

Checking information test

Look at the two lists below and check to see whether the information in List A has been correctly transferred to List B. If there is a mistake in column A, mark circle A on your answer sheet. If there is a mistake in column B, mark circle B on your answer sheet. If there is a mistake in column C, mark circle C on your answer sheet. If there is a mistake in column D, mark circle D on your answer sheet. If there are no errors in that line, mark circle E on your answer sheet. Note that there may be more than one error in a line.

LIST A

A Date	B Name	C Time	D Ref Num
12.1	Williams	13.30	2613
3.8	Chan	07.29	5971

LIST B

A Date	B Name	C Time	D Ref Num
Jan 12	WILLIAMS	15:30	3612
March 8	CHAN	09:27	579

Answers Checking Information

1=DE

2=CE

Working with numbers/Numerical Reasoning Test

(to be done without using a calculator)

1. How much will five tins of soup cost at 55p a tin?

A	B	C	D	E
£2.25	£2.55	£2.60	£2.75	£2.95

2. A person saves £35 in four weeks. At this rate how much will have been saved in one year?

A	B	C	D	E
£200	£250	£355	£420	£455

3. What is the total cost of a journey when £1.65 is spent on bus-fares and an Underground ticket costs £2.50?

A	B	C	D	E
£3.15	£3.60	£3.95	£4.05	£4.15

4. What is the average number of people per car, when six cars carry thirty people?

A	B	C	D	E

4.5   5.0   5.5   6.0   6.5

5. If shopping items cost £12.64, how much money remains out of £20?

A   B   C   D   E

£6.36   £6.63   £7.36   £7.46   £7.63

Answers working with numbers

1=D

2=E

3=E

4=B

5=C

Verbal/logical reasoning test
Some time on the night of 4th November, the Zanzibar Club was burnt to the ground. The Police are treating the fire as suspicious. The only facts known at this stage are:
• The club was insured for more than its real value.

• The club belonged to Jim Tuttle.

• David Braithwaite was known to dislike Jim Tuttle.

• Between 3rd November and 4th November, David Braithwaite was away from home on a business trip.

• There were no fatalities.

• A plan of the club was found in David Braithwaite's flat.

A = TRUE B = FALSE C = IMPOSSIBLE TO SAY

1. A member of Jim Tuttle's family died in the blaze.

A B C

2. If the insurance company pays out in full, Jim Tuttle stands to profit from the fire.

A B C

3. The flat where the plan was found is close to the club.

A B C

4. Jim Tuttle could have been at the club when the fire took place.

A B C

5. There are definite grounds to arrest David Braithwaite for arson.

A B C

Answers Verbal Reasoning

1=B

2=A

3=C

4=A

5=B

What can you do to give your best performance?

Don't be down-hearted if you find the questions difficult or get a lot of them wrong. There are many things you can do to improve your performance. Practice is one answer, another is to simply slow down and take your time. The tests are not designed for you to be able to completely finish them. It merely assesses that you can undertake tasks efficiently and to a set standard.

Practice doing simple arithmetic without using a calculator. Do number puzzles. Do the scoring when playing games such as darts, card games etc. Put a ruler or something similar with a straight edge under lists. Take a few deep breaths before you start and don't try to rush.

Make sure that you know what you have to do before you start putting pencil to paper – if you do not understand, ask the person who is administering the test.

Read the instructions carefully before each test starts in order to make sure that you understand. Don't skim through them – you may overlook important details and in consequence make mistakes you could have avoided.

Even if you have taken the test before, don't assume that the instructions (and the worked examples) are the same as the last time – they may have changed.

Once the test begins work as quickly and as accurately as you can. Choose an easy to answer question first to boost confidence.

Avoid spending too much time on questions you find difficult. Find an easier question then go back later if you have time.

If you are uncertain about an answer, enter you best reasoned choice (but avoid simply guessing).

If you have some spare time after you have answered all questions, go back and check through your answers.

Keep working as hard as you can throughout the test – the more correct answers you get the higher your score will be.

Be positive in your attitude. Previous failures in tests or examinations are in the past and you should not allow that to have a detrimental effect on your performance on this occasion. Focus and believe you can pass the test.

The person who interviews you will assess your responses against the type of behaviours you need for the role of a Police officer against the seven core competancies. So that you can do your best make sure you are familiar with the competencies and that your answer gives you an opportunity to explain how you have shown this behaviour fully.

Fitness Test
The fitness test will test your dynamic strength, which involves performing five seated chest pushes and five seated back pulls on the dyno machine to measure your strength.

The second part is the endurance part where you will be asked to run to and fro along a 15 metre track in time with a series of bleeps, which become increasingly faster. You can retake your fitness test up to three times.

The Final Interview
The final force interview if your chosen force does a final interview. This is where you get a chance to be yourself and also ask questions as well as questions being asked of you. You may well be asked why you want to be a police officer and your career aspirations. Try not to use the usual "to fight crime" it should be more about supporting your local community and making a difference within the community. Being a police officer is now very much community and customer focused.

Try to relax and just be yourself answering questions with some detail but try not to waffle. There are no questions to try and trip you up but questions to explore your experience your attitudes and the type of person you are. This is why it is so important to "just be plain you".

TRAINING

You have passed all the tests and the interview and your final security clearance has been done, you will now receive a date for your training. What will you learn? What will you do? How long will it last?

Training is a vital part of becoming a police officer. It is a very wide ranging job and requires, for example, knowledge of the law, to be able to undertake the job effectively. Don't expect even after training to just walk out onto the beat and have all the knowledge and experience you need. It takes many years to build this up and it is all too easy to get frustrated by your lack of knowledge at times. Experience with dealing with a wide range of offences and incidents will slowly build up your knowledge. A good tutor constable will aid your initial learning period on patrol. Later on you will work with other police officers to give you a good insight into how different officers do their jobs. Once signed off for independent patrol you can attend incidents on your own and be single crewed. That first time out on your own is a little harrowing but at the same time, a sense of achievement that you are thought to be competent enough to work independently. From there on in, the learning never stops. As you attend a plethora of incidents and learn something from each one.

Probation is the first step in your career and this lasts for two years or usually one year for a Special Constable. This is a time where training is intensive and progress is carefully monitored. You will get every assistance to build the skills you'll need as an officer - and when you complete the probationary period, you'll become a Police Constable or Special Constable. Training's carried out at a force training centre or maybe an affiliated college depending on the force. Special Constable Training is nearly always carried out at the force's training centre.

Probation's all about continuous professional development - and the first step is induction training. Some forces you'll be issued with your uniform, shown how to maintain it, advised about conditions of service. You will then start an initial phase of training looking at procedures and some aspects of law. Officer Safety Training will also help you deal with confrontational or violent situations and is a mandatory requirement for you to be allowed to go out on patrol with your tutor Constable for both Regular and Special Constables.

Special Constable Training

Special Constables have a much shorter and more intensive training program. With the length of the course they do not cover everything a full-time officer would. Law is one element that is greatly reduced and the training is there to cover the more basic policing role that Special Constable's are normally expected to undertake. Much of what a Special Constable will learn certainly as they progress in service will be learnt on the street from other officers and maybe attending more specialised training.

Below is an outline and content for a typical force training course. They do vary but the content for all is very similar and it's mainly the order that changes.

The first weekend will be designed to introduce you to the force you will be working with and to gain an understanding of policing. This should give you a good grasp of how the force works and what they are trying to achieve. You will learn about the force's aims and policing style and about providing a service that meets the needs of everyone in the community. You may also look at how being a Special Constable affects your life and what being a Special Constable means to you and your family. You will be given the opportunity to discuss with your intake your hopes and fears about becoming a Special. You may well make some lifelong friends along the way. You will also be taken through important issues such as health and safety.

On the second, third and fourth weekends you will receive your Officer Safety Training (OST), which will give you the skills you need to deal with situations on the street. You cover first aid and Unarmed Defence Tactics (UDT) and your Personal Protective Equipment (PPE), like handcuffs, and other force-specific equipment such as the side arm baton, ASP baton and CS or PAVA spray. These weekends will be physically demanding and may be challenging at first.

UDT consists of tactics designed to defend you from attack and techniques to help restrain or move an offender.

Handcuff training will take you through the basic techniques needed to handcuff somebody as well as different types of handcuffing.

CS/PAVA, here you will use an inert CS/PAVA spray filled with water to practice drawing and aiming the spray on an individual and group.

ASP training involves techniques for using the ASP baton both extended and closed, as well as going through the safe areas on the body that that baton can be used on. Training on the side arm baton is also very similar.

You go through the technique and circumstances for using leg restraints, how best to deploy them and the potential risk of leaving them on too long.

The final weekends will provide you with the legal knowledge you require to start your job out on the streets. The legislation you learn will prove invaluable and is just the beginning – from this point you will always be learning and gaining knowledge about criminal legislation and looking at specific offences. Not only will you be revising your law, but you will also be taking part in role-play exercises and learning how to use radios and deal with real-life scenarios. You will also look at diversity, basic use of force, IT systems, filling in crime reports and recording witness statements as well as how to use your pocket note book.

Regular Officer Training
An example of a typical Initial Police Learning and Development Programme (IPLDP) course might consist of:

PHASE 1 – INTRODUCTION

For the first phase of training, you will spend 3 weeks on this section

The modules covered in this phase include:

- health and safety

- first aid

- race and diversity

- ethics and values

- information technology

- problem solving

- team working.

You will also have 3 days of basic personal safety training and start looking at social, community and neighborhood policing in order to prepare you for the next phase of your training.

PHASE 2 - COMMUNITY ENGAGEMENT

You will spend two weeks in a Professional Development Unit (PDU) you will get to know your tutor and supervisor as well as the PDU staff and station and be given information about the local community make-up and the role the local Police play.

You will spend the remainder of time with a local community group.

PHASE 3(A)- LEGISLATION,PROCEDURES AND GUIDELINES

This phase is for 12 weeks. You will be given the knowledge you need to go out on supervised patrol and members of the community may attend as guest speakers or role players.

This phase also include a day of Police Support Unit training and the rest of your personal safety and information technology training. You will then have one week's holiday.

PHASE 3 (B) SUPERVISED PATROL

This is for 12 weeks and takes place at one of the PDUs. You will be assigned a tutor on a one to one basis who will support you for the remainder of your probation.

During this phase of the training you will be given time to complete your Student Officer Learning and Development Portfolio (SOLAP) or Professional Development Portfolio (PDP). You will also attend a one week classroom based course where you will be taught the legislation on subjects such as Anti-Social Behaviour Orders (ASBOs) using live local data.

At the end of the 12 weeks you will be ready to go out on independent patrol.

PHASE 4 - INDEPENDENT PATROL

This is for 4 weeks and is based at your PDU. If your area has a neighborhood policing scheme, then you will also spend some time on that.

Either before or during your training you will be attested which is where you are sworn in as Constable by taking an oath with a magistrate or justice of the peace present.

Foundation Degree
Other forces have brought in training that leads to a qualification such as a foundation degree. This is to support a police officer as a professional with professional qualifications in a similar vain to a teacher or doctor.
You are will be enrolled onto a Foundation Degree in Policing with an affiliated university.

The aim is to provide student officers with the initial education and training required not only to meet levels of professional competence, but also provide the breadth of knowledge and gain a recognized qualification.

The Foundation Degree in Policing is an integral part of the IPLDP and is usually delivered jointly by the force you are training with and at a university of college site.

Like any study it does demand effort, commitment and time with various written assignments and the odd phase test.

The Modules of a typical program

The modules are as follows:

Year 1

Law, Procedure and Professional Judgement

Community Engagement and Diversity Awareness 1

Policing in Practice 1

Policing Theory and Organisation 1

Police Study and Development Skills

Year 2

Community Engagement and Diversity Awareness 2

Policing in Practice 2

Policing Theory and Organisation 2.

In order to be confirmed in post as a Police Constable after the two years of the force will expect you to have successfully completed all the modules.

The way the course is delivered encompasses a variety of teaching techniques to allow for the different learning styles of student officers.

• Group discussions

• Group work

• Role-plays

• Self directed learning

• Individual tutorials

• Negotiated community visits

• Community placement

• Workplace mentoring (tutoring)

• Workshops

Personal study is an integral part of the course and will take the form of directed reading, self-study and preparation for assignments. In addition to the face-to-face tuition and group sessions at the training venues, the course may also make use of electronic learning via systems such as Moodle or police online learning systems.

OATH

One of the first things you do after joining as a police officer be it a regular officer or special is to be attested. In simple terms it is basically saying an oath to be sworn in as a police officer.

English Oath "I, ..(your name) .. of ..(your force) .. do solemnly and sincerely declare and affirm that I will well and truly serve the Queen in the office of Constable, with fairness, integrity, diligence and impartiality, upholding fundamental human rights and according equal respect to all people; and that I will, to the best of my power, cause the peace to be kept and preserved and prevent all offences against people and property; and that while I continue to hold the said office I will to the best of my skill and knowledge discharge all the duties thereof faithfully according to law."

Welsh Oath "Rwyf i...o...yn datgan ac yn cadarnhau yn ddifrifol ac yn ddiffuant y byddaf yn gwasanaethu'r Frenhines yn dda ac yn gywir yn fy swydd o heddwas (heddferch), yn deg, yn onest, yn ddiwyd ac yn ddiduedd, gan gynnal hawliau dynol sylfaenol a chan roddi'r un parch i bob person; ac y byddaf i, hyd eithaf fy ngallu, yn achosi i'r heddwch gael ei gadw a'i ddiogelu ac yn atal pob trosedd yn erbyn pobl ac eiddo; a thra byddaf yn parhau i ddal y swydd ddywededig y byddaf i, hyd eithaf fy sgil a'm gwybodaeth, yn cyflawni'r holl ddyletswyddau sy'n gysylltiedig â hi yn ffyddlon yn unol â'r gyfraith."

Scotland has no specific words that are prescribed within current Scottish Police legislation. Section 16 of the Police (Scotland) act 1967 merely requires that "A person appointed to the office of Constable in a police force shall on appointment make, before a sheriff (or justice of the peace), a declaration in such terms as may be prescribed concerning the proper discharge of the duties of the office." The declaration is typically given in the form:

"I hereby do solemnly and sincerely declare and affirm that I will faithfully discharge the duties of the office of Constable/Special Constable."

Once attested you are entitled to your warrant card this may be issued any time during your initial training phase but before you go out on duty and identifies yourself as a Police officer.

Most forces use experiential learning; as the name suggests you learn from experience. The full cycle is to reflect on your experience and Interpret. This is trying to make sense of an event and compiling an action plan for the future .Perhaps it is just like playing a computer game where you have a crash or get killed; you think about it and try it again, maybe changing the way you did it originally.

Training will aim to provide you with the skills and expertise you need to carry out a number of core tasks that will be built into your probation period.

IT Training IT is used by all forces for various systems for doing things like recording crime, gathering intelligence, briefing, and showing incidents within the force. Being able to use packages such as Microsoft Word for word processing reports, statements and Microsoft Outlook for Email will be of use.

Probation is about 2 years. It is during this period that you and the force can assess whether the Police Force is right for you and you feel it is the right choice as well.

Most of the ongoing training you need will be delivered in the policing district or area where you work. It will involve a mixture of practical training and further lessons on subjects such as law updates, IT updates, scenes of crime preservation, Victim care and diversity.

All forces have an ongoing training schedule, so that you can learn a new skill or update existing skills. Your force or division will have a training plan in place with dates for training. Some training like UDT, CS, and handcuffs etc is mandatory training that you have to take and re-qualify at least once a year.

Regular officers have to complete a PDP or SOLAP while they are on probation. The aim is to collate evidence about your work to show that you have gained experience in all of the core tasks. The Portfolio will contain information such as reports from supervisors, records of attendance on training courses, law notes and other evidence about the work you have carried out. Keeping the profile up to date is the responsibility of individual officers. It does help to see what you have done and what you need to do to complete your probation period.

Key areas you may cover once at your allocated station are:

In the police station the police station front desk is often where the first point of contact between the police and public takes place. You will learn how to handle enquiries appropriately and effectively, giving advice, taking down information or referring people on to someone who can help.

Dealing with traffic road safety is an important concern for the Police and it is quite likely you will be involved in enforcing traffic law. You will need to know what action you should take and when. You may also be involved in dealing with traffic collisions (RTC) and will need to know how to protect the scene, control traffic and locate and identify witnesses.

Dealing with incidents being a uniformed officer on patrol you may be the first to arrive at the scene of an incident. Whether it is a domestic dispute or a burglary, you will be expected to know what to do. You will be taught how to establish what has happened, who needs to be informed and how to control the scene. It takes time and experience to become proficient, which is why you spend so much time with a tutor Constable and then continue to work with an experienced officer until you are deemed fit to go out on independent patrol.

Making an arrest there will be times when you have to arrest a suspect or help other officers make an arrest. Ensuring your safety and that of the people around you will involve knowledge of restraint techniques, how to use equipment such as CS spray and a baton to apply appropriate force. A good legal knowledge of your powers to make an arrest is essential. You will cover some of the basics in the next chapter. You will be taught how to escort detainees to the custody centre and how to search them.

Investigating Another important aspect is the investigation of a crime and obtaining full and accurate statements from victims and witnesses. You will receive instruction on how to take statements and how to write your own if you have been a witness.

Patrolling If patrolling is to be effective, it needs to be well planned and well executed. You will learn about planning a patrol to meet the particular needs of your beat and to tackle the fear of crime. You will need to establish a good network of contacts throughout the community and use the information they give to provide a better policing service on your patch. You will also learn practical skills such as using correct radio procedures by actually going out on the beat.

Driving As a police officer you will be expected to drive and Police Forces have a wide variety of vehicles from arctic lorries to a JCB. You start off with a standard license to drive marked and unmarked cars up to a set power limit set by the force. You can then undertake further advanced course to be able to use blue lights, then a pursuit course to drive higher power car's and be able to undertake pursuits. You can also do courses for van driving, motorcycle and various other vehicles the force may have. The Association Chief Police Officers (APCO) has guidelines for the Police Driving competences, which set out the national standards for Police Driving. Very few Forces allow Special Constables to have anything more than Standard and Van driving on their Police licence.

Police Standard Driving

Element 1: Vehicle preparation

Performance criteria

a. The roadworthiness of the vehicle is established.

b. The physical and mental fitness of the driver is established.

c. Defects or faults relating to the roadworthiness of the vehicle

are:

_ identified

_ recorded

_ remedied.

d. Ensure vehicle is properly equipped for operational purposes.

e. Defects relating to vehicle equipment are:

_ identified

_ recorded

_ remedied.

Element 2: Use of vehicle

Performance criteria

a. Perform pre-drive check.

b. Plan, prioritise and justify use of the vehicle at all times.

c. The vehicle is driven within:

_ driver's personal limitations

_ vehicle limitations.

d. The vehicle is driven in a professional manner by:

_ displaying consideration for others

_ minimising wear and tear and risk of accidental damage

_ operating all vehicle controls smoothly and accurately

_ recognising hazards and potential hazards and implement

the 'Roadcraft' system of control accordingly

_ understanding the causes of skidding and demonstrate how to correct them

_ adopting the best road position at all times

_ using signals when necessary and act upon the signals of other road users

_ negotiating corners and bends, having correctly assessed their severity

_ overtaking and rejoining their own side of the road in plenty of time.

e. Observe potential hazards and react accordingly.

Police Advanced Driving

Element 1: Advanced driver high-speed situations

Performance criteria

a. Accurately identify the need for high-speed response to any incident.

b. Drive within vehicle limitations and characteristics.

c. Anticipate and respond to behaviour of other road users who may not be able to judge speed of Police vehicles.

d. Constantly assess the maintenance of high-speed response through extended observation skills.

e. Verbalise progress through accurate and measured commentary.

Element 2: Advanced driver response to incidents

Performance criteria

a. Stabilise emotional/physical effects of continued high-speed driving in relation to incident requirements.

b. Know how to position vehicle in a safe relationship to the incident/circumstances.

Element 3: Advanced driver essential attitudes

Performance criteria

a. Recognise the need to give priority to public safety.

b. Recognise the need to place safety above the desire to apprehend a suspect.

c. Give priority, at all times, to safety over the desire to attend an incident.

d. Control at all times, while driving, the competitive urge.

e. During journey concentrate solely on safe driving.

f. Recognise fatigue and personal stress levels which may affect judgment and respond accordingly.

g. Recognise that adrenaline may impair judgment

Element 4: Driving skills - car control

Performance criteria

a. Demonstrate and apply correct steering techniques in a smooth controlled manner.

b. Adapt steering techniques while reversing.

c. Change gear smoothly, using correct technique, at the appropriate time (always in the correct gear according to the speed of the vehicle).

d. Accurately assess and use the correct degree of acceleration.

e. Accelerate and decelerate accurately and smoothly.

f. Understand the effect of braking in relation to weight distribution and vehicle handling.

g. Apply and release foot brake at correct time, in a proficient smooth manner.

h. Understand the limits of the braking system while reversing.

i. Understand the basics of anti-lock braking systems.

j. Use of the handbrake at the correct times and in the appropriate manner.

k. Understand the basics of traction control.

Element 5: Driving skills - system of car control

Performance criteria

a. Demonstrate a thorough understanding of the 'Police System of Car Control' as defined in the Roadcraft Manual.

b. Apply the system of car control at all times.

c. Observe and correctly interpret all potential hazards and Act accordingly.

d. Adjust driving to circumstances developing around vehicle.

e. Take appropriate action to cope with any hazard while maintaining complete control of vehicle.

Element 6: Driving skills - positioning

Performance criteria

a. Correctly position vehicle on the road in all circumstances.

b. When following other vehicles take up the safest/correct

position for:

_ bends

_ roundabouts

_ dual-carriageways/motorways

_ overtaking

_ junctions.

Element 7: Driving skills - overtaking

Performance criteria

a. Make progress safely.

b. Overtake safely at all times.

c. Make accurate judgments when overtaking stationary and moving vehicles.

d. Precisely plan and execute overtaking manoeuvres.

e. Judge and use speed correctly at all times.

f. Take into account potential dangers and adjust speed accordingly.

g. Be aware of speed, its effects and the capabilities and limitations of the vehicle being driven.

Element 8: Driving skills - general

Performance criteria

a. Demonstrates ability to give concise, accurate commentaries while maintaining the required driving standard.

b. Capable of parking the vehicle close to the kerb in all circumstances without inconvenience to other road users.

c. Capable of reversing a vehicle with restricted rear visibility by using the exterior mirrors.

d. Able to identify quickly the type and cause of a skid.

e. Demonstrates the ability to control each type of skid effectively.

f. Demonstrates the ability to stop a skidding vehicle using different braking techniques while remaining in control of the vehicle.

g. Demonstrates the ability to drive safely on a slippery road.

h. Drives vehicles without causing unnecessary wear by paying attention to tyres, engine, clutch and bodywork.

PURSUIT DRIVING

Element 1: Pursuit initiation

Performance criteria

a. Consider 'safety' to be the priority and abandon pursuit if circumstances dictate.

b. Give priority, at all times, to safety over the desire to continue a pursuit.

c. Inform control room of commencement of the pursuit.

d. Maintain accurate and effective commentary to a detached control room and other sources.

e. Request supporting resources as necessary.

f. Take responsibilities of ground commander when appropriate.

Element 2: Pursuit evaluation

Performance criteria

a. Decide whether to initiate a pursuit having considered ACPO criteria.

b. Review options available.

c. Consider whether road, traffic and weather conditions make 'pursuit' a valid option.

d. Assess suitability of vehicle for the particular pursuit.

e. Assess whether personal driving skills are adequate for the circumstances.

f. Consider your present physical and mental capabilities to participate in a pursuit.

g. Remain objective while evaluating the situation, keeping competitive instincts under control.

Element 3: Pursuit driving

Performance criteria

a. Driver constantly assesses the risk of continuing to pursue and abandons if dangerous.

b. Maintains radio contact and commentary in prescribed format.

 c. Follows at a safe distance, declines any form of challenge from suspect, remains cool, resists temptation to overtake.

d. Uses agreed procedures to safely bring pursuit to a conclusion.

e. Constantly reviews the need to rely on Road Traffic Act exemption.

Element 4: Pursuit conclusion

Performance criteria

a. Give or arrange medical attention to injured persons if necessary.

b. Obtain other emergency resources if required.

c. Preserve evidence where necessary.

d. Accurately record details while fresh in memory.

e. Review and reflect on the whole pursuit.

f. Prepare reports.

g. Make recommendations for changing policy, practice procedure.

h. Attend debrief and actively contribute.

ON DUTY

It is your first time on duty and in uniform, what can you expect to do? How will you know what to do? The first time you go out in uniform it is a little nerve-racking but you will soon settle down and your tutor Constable will go through what you need to do. We will start this chapter by looking at what you might do on an average shift. Don't worry if you don't understand all the terminology, you will later on.

02:30pm Arrive at Police station and change into uniform.

02:45pm Go into parade room and get my radio and CS spray and any other kit I require.

03:00pm Go into a briefing with shift. The Shift sergeant leads the briefing and goes through recent events and priorities for the shift. High visible patrol in burglary hotspots, town centre patrol, checking parks for teenagers who are drinking. At the briefing everyone is paired up and allocated call sign i.e. BW66, CB57 or AB24.

03:30pm I have some initial paperwork to complete before going out a couple of tickets need posting and I have a file to complete ready for an interview tomorrow

04:30pm Get keys to a car and go out on patrol.

05:00pm I pull a car over and issue a fixed penalty notice for using a mobile phone whilst driving.

6:30pm Now out patrolling the town centre I have been joined by a Special Constable who I regularly work with, talking to local pub door staff when the first radio call comes in. A group of teenagers are causing a disturbance outside a fish and chip shop so we go off to investigate.

6:40pm We arrive at the scene of the disturbance to find a group of 12 teenagers throwing chips and generally being rowdy. We stop and have a chat and use the stop check forms to check details. A couple of them do have previous cases of theft but nothing current. After giving a verbal warning, we ask them to move on.

7:00pm Back on the patrol, we decide to do a walk through the parks which are just being locked up for the night. A couple of people are making their way to the exit.

7:30pm We have another call about a group of teenagers drinking and being noisy in the park. The description given fits that of the group we spoke to earlier outside the chip shop. We make our way to the park.

7:40pm On entering the park some of the group start to run so we pick up the pace a little and manage to catch up with nearly all of the group before they have chance to climb over the fence. A few of the group are drunk and two are holding opened bottles of wine and lager. From the previous checks at the chip shop we know they are all under age so the opened alcohol is seized and poured away. They are warned that they are trespassing, as the park is now closed. One male, who is drunk, becomes abusive and starts to swear and he is given a section 5 warning. One girl is heavily drunk and can barely walk so a decision is made that she needs escorting home. We request another unit to our location to assist. Our male continues to swear and is given a second and final section 5 public order warning.

Another unit arrives and takes the very drunk female home for her personal safety. We then disperse the rest of the group after giving them all a final warning and they are told to go home.

7:55pm We follow the group out and as we get over the fence the male who swore at us drops his trousers in the distance so we give chase; although he is quick we catch up with him. He is then cautioned and arrested for indecent exposure and being drunk and disorderly. Being on foot patrol, we need to request a van to come and pick him up. We then convey the male to custody where he is booked in and details given. As he is drunk we cannot interview him about the offence so we will need to do a handover pack for the morning shift to be able to deal with it.

8:30pm Back at the Police station we undertake the paperwork for the arrest. This includes an arrest statement as to why and under what circumstances the arrest was made. The crime reporting paperwork and handover pack needs compiling and that includes all the paperwork that the morning shift will need to continue the investigation and see if he can be charged.

09:30pm A call comes in with reports of a fight outside a pub. As it is an immediate we are authorised to use the blue lights and quickly get to the fight. On arrival there is nothing to be seen; a few people walking to taxis and to the various takeaways but nobody matching the description. We talk to the door staff and they have not seen anything either. We then get back into the car and do an area search to see if we can find any of the offenders, but there is no trace. With that call-out checked we resume patrol work.

09:45pm The next call reports domestic violence at a house. We put on the blue lights. On arrival there is still some shouting going on and the door is slightly open. We enter the property to find the couple still arguing, so we part them and take one into the kitchen and one into the living room to try and ascertain what has happened. Both have been drinking and the fight is down to the mother-in-law coming to stay the next day. Both parties are still quite emotional and as soon as they catch sight of each other start to argue. As we feel there could be further breaches of the peace we ask if the male can go and stay somewhere else for the night. He replies he can go to a mate's house so we offer to take him there to make sure he does not go back to his home address.

10:30pm Back on patrol. We will have some paperwork to do for the domestic fight we have just been to but for the moment, on a busy Friday night, the greater need is to be on patrol and available for jobs as they come in.

10:45pm The third call comes in asking us to go to a driver, possibly drunk and seen wandering across the road. We head off and follow the car, checking its details and pull the car over using the blue lights. I go round and ask the driver to step out of the car whilst my colleague gets the breathalyser out. I can smell alcohol on the man's breath and on breathalysing him he is over the legal limit. He is duly cautioned and arrested for drink driving and then conveyed to custody. Once booked in to custody we take him to the intoxylyser for further samples of breath and on both readings he is twice the legal limit of 35mg at 70mg. He is then taken back to the cells to be charged in the morning.

00:30am Finally all paperwork is complete and time to book off duty and go home should have finished at 12 but we cannot go off duty until all the paperwork needed by the morning shift is completed for our arrests.

As can be seen, whilst on duty you can come across a whole variety of incidents and crimes and no two shifts are ever the same. You never stop coming across new incidents and never stop learning.

Equipment

Going out on the beat does require you to have various bits of equipment for protection known as PPE and equipment to gather and record information. Equipment does vary from force to force.

Pocket Note Book - this low tech piece of equipment is one of the most important. Some forces make greater use of it than others do. It is a legal document that can be used in court and outlines what you have done each time you are on duty: it can be used to record details of incidents and take brief statements.

Blackberry – More and more frontline officers are equipped with smartphones the most common one being issued is the blackberry. These can be used as normal mobile phones/smart phones. They also have the capability for officers to do PNC checks, do crime reports, add intelligence, and other information onto the various police systems. Being a mobile phone they do suffer they same issues as any other mobile phone in turns of reception and data speeds.

Torch - this is essential for helping to search at night or even during the day in unlit buildings or a dark area within a car like under the seats.

Stab Vest - the Police Patrol body armour style has been designed to provide you with a light and easy to wear stab proof vest. The item is made in hard-wearing poly cotton fabric and supplied with epaulettes, radio loops and two large utility pockets. The inserts are made of Kevlar and consist of one at the front, one at the back and two in each of the shoulders. It's imperative that it is fitted correctly and zipped up fully to give maximum protection.

Utility Belt- if issued holds all your personal equipment outlined below. It can also hold a first aid kit and have pockets to hold paperwork such as stop search forms or fixed penalty notices.

CS Spray - CS spray is classed as a firearm and can only be stored securely at the Police station and used by a trained officer whilst on duty.

The CS is in the form of a hand-held aerosol canister, with the solution being 5% CS, with Methyl isobutyl ketone, which is propelled by Nitrogen. The liquid stream is directed where the user points the canister, and is accurate up to 4 meters. It has been noted that the solvent MiBK that the CS is suspended in, is itself harmful, and can cause inflammation, dermatitis, burns to the skin and liver damage in isolated cases.

PAVA spray - this is used by some forces, and others have been trialing its use. It is dispensed from a hand-held canister similar to CS spray, in a liquid stream that contains a 0.3% solution of

PAVA (Pelargonic Acid Vanillylamide) in a solvent of aqueous ethanol. The propellant is nitrogen the same as CS spray.

This solution has been selected because this is the minimum concentration which will fulfill the purpose of the equipment; namely to minimise a person's capacity for resistance without unnecessarily prolonging their discomfort. It should be noted that PAVA is significantly more potent than CS.

The liquid stream is a spray pattern and has a maximum effective range of up to 4 meters. Maximum accuracy, however, will be achieved over a distance of 1.25 - 2 meters. The operating distance is the distance between the canister and the subject's eyes, not the distance between the officer and the subject.

Limb Restraint – this is used by many forces now as a way to restrain offenders. The straps come as a pair and are wound round the ankle and just below the knee and held together with strong Velcro. They reduce the risk of the offender being able to kick at officers as they are placed into a prison van or Police car.

ASP - a tactical baton that works by using a friction lock system of telescopic tubes, which can be deployed almost instantly. This allows the ASP to quickly extend at the flick of the wrist. It can be used either extended or retracted and also works as a visual deterrent. It should only be used where appropriate force is required or as a defence when searching a property or area where offenders could be present. The ASP can also be used to break windows to gain access to properties or vehicles.

Radio - all Police forces use the Airwave system, which is a secure digital communication system that offers many benefits, such as the ability to talk directly with other officers (point to point), text and use GPS and have an emergency button that will give you air priority if you need it. They are very similar in operation to, and look like, mobile phones. Sepura are one major supplier and Motorolla another.

Handcuffs - restraint devices designed to secure an individual's wrists close together. Speed cuffs are used by most forces and are handcuffs made by Hiatt & Company. They are characterised by their rigid design, the two cuffs being joined by a rigid metal bar and a black plastic grip, replacing the chain of earlier types of cuff. Their rigidity and the design of the grip makes them effective for gaining control over a struggling prisoner even if only one cuff has been applied.

Paperwork - part of Police work is doing various form filling or paperwork. Some of this paperwork you may carry with you, such as stop search forms or Fixed Penalty Notices - all forces have a wide variety of paperwork for associated crimes and incidents. The exact layout and procedure does vary from force to force. It is worth getting to know the more commonly used ones.

Radio Usage

Using the radio can seem a little scary at first. What do I say? How do I say it? Again radio protocol does vary from force to force. The phonetic alphabet (used to spell out words or give registration numbers) is used throughout all forces. Outlined below is the phonetic alphabet and it is worth learning.

A	Alpha (or "Alfa")
B	Bravo
C	Charlie
D	Delta
E	Echo
F	Foxtrot
G	Golf
H	Hotel
I	India
J	Juliet (or "Juliett")
K	Kilo
L	Lima
M	Mike
N	November
O	Oscar
P	Papa
Q	Quebec

R	Romeo
S	Sierra
T	Tango
U	Uniform
V	Victor
W	Whisky
X	X-Ray
Y	Yankee
Z	Zulu

A large proportion of radio usage is operational and varies from force to force and so cannot really be put into this book for security reasons. But the best way to learn how to use the radio is listen to how existing regular Police officers use theirs and you will be amazed at how quickly you pick it up. The radio is the main device used to deploy officers.

A central control room will direct officers to the various jobs. Often these are graded due to their nature and importance. A red job or immediate for instance is an emergency, usually given when there is a risk to life or property and allows immediate response with the use of blue lights. Other jobs may not pose an immediate threat but still require a response within an hour, those that are then graded as even lower may require a police presence within 24 hours. Lower grade jobs may include some anti-social behavior, a theft were nothing was seen or heard and no description of an offender, an assault that happened on a previous day or much earlier time than reported. The grading is often based around either a crime being in progress or an offender on the scene. All forces have their own requirements for grading of jobs.

To the customer or victim when they ring the police to report something it will always be of high importance to them. As a police officer you often have to manage their expectations and explain the course of action and why you will carry out that action.

MoPI

MoPI (Management of Police Information) work stream represents a huge programme of policy, process and cultural change across the whole of the police organisation. Any police force works on intelligence and ensuring it collects and disseminated data to the relevant and authorised people. Any force has various systems for collecting data, be it Memmex for intelligence or CRMS for the recording and reporting of crimes. It is essential that all this data can be linked and shared with other forces or agencies. The data also needs to be relevant and fit for purpose and data no longer needed or relevant is disposed of.

MoPI has been implemented by all police forces in England and Wales. Most forces have achieved the targets they set for themselves through their local MoPI action plans to ensure they manage information effectively and efficiently. MoPI is now business as usual to ensure continuity in the management of information. MoPI supports national standards across the police service. MoPI is about making information relevant and accessible; ensuring that all police operational information is managed effectively. MoPI covers the whole of the information life cycle, through collection & recording, evaluation, sharing and review, retention & disposal.

MoPI Code of Practice

The murder of Holly Wells and Jessica Chapman in August 2002 by Ian Huntley and the subsequent inquiry by Sir Michael Bichard had a profound and far reaching effect on how the police service now gathers, manages, use and shares information. As a result of the inquiry, in 2005 the home secretary issued a statuary code of practice on the management of police information this then became referred to as MoPI.

The code insures that:

Should only be retained if required for a 'Policing Purpose'
Should be grouped according to the nature of the information

Must undergo a Review/Retention and deletion process after a period of time commensurate with the nature of the information.

This code is intended to:

Ensure that information is managed consistently, throughout its entire lifecycle.

Allow information known about individuals to be readily identified and shared between police agencies across the UK.

Create a consistent national standard.

Help develop national information with the PND (Police National Database).

Power of Arrest

As a police officer in England or Wales you have the power to arrest a person within England and Wales. If you are a police officer in Scotland then your arrest power only extends to Scotland. This power of arrest is:

"Arrest is the apprehending or restraining of a person in order to detain him at the police station while the alleged or suspected crime is investigated and in order that he be forthcoming to answer an alleged or suspected crime."

The most important reason, but not the only reason, for the suspect being arrested is to allow him to be questioned about the offence of which he is suspected. Other reasons for arresting a person include the prevention of a breach of the peace or the protection of that person from harm while they are drunk or mentally ill.

A Police officer has wide powers of arrest under s24 Police and Criminal Evidence Act 1984. A lawful arrest requires two distinct elements :(a) Suspected or has attempted involvement in the commission of a criminal offence; and

(b) Compliance with the necessity test.

A Miranda warning, known as the "Caution", is a warning given by police to criminal suspects in police custody, or in a custodial situation, before they are questioned. A custodial situation is one in which the suspect's freedom of movement is restrained although they are not under arrest.

An arrest begins with what the person is being arrested for e.g. I am arresting you for section 5 public order, theft of a bottle of wine or ABH (actual bodily harm), this is followed by the caution :

"You do not have to say anything. But it may harm your defence if you do not mention when questioned something which you later rely on in court. Anything you do say may be given in evidence."

The caution above is worth learning and should roll off your tongue as and when it is required.

At this point it is important to mention human rights, which apply during arrest, detention and in the interview process. Human rights apply as they do in our day to day lives. The Human Rights Act 1998 sets out the rights in the UK which are protected by the European Convention on Human Rights (ECHR).

The act did not invent human rights for British people; instead, it introduced into our domestic law some of the rights set out in the Universal Declaration of Human Rights and other international documents.

More specifically, it gave greater effect within the UK to the rights and freedoms protected by the ECHR, a treaty that British lawyers helped to draft. The main part of human rights is the belief that everybody should be treated equally and with dignity, no matter what their circumstances.

This means that nobody should be tortured or treated in an inhuman or degrading way. It also means that everybody should have access to public services and the right to be treated fairly by those services. This applies to all public services, including the criminal justice system. If you arrest someone and they are charged, they should not be treated with prejudice and their trial should be fair. Another example is if you arrest someone for shop theft you should not parade them through the store unless you have no alternative.

UK law includes a range of human rights which protect us from poor treatment and prejudice, and which require everyone to have equal and fair treatment from public authorities.

Reasonable Force
Police officers are empowered by common law and statute to use force to protect life, preserve order, prevent the commission of crime or arrest or detain offenders. Common law powers are afforded also to all members of the general public.

Use of reasonable force by a police officer must be, proportionate, reasonable in the circumstances and the minimum amount necessary to accomplish the lawful objective concerned. Persons being taken into police custody should not have greater force used towards them than is required to achieve restraint. Force should not be used in a manner that is arbitrary, unreasonable or based on irrational considerations. This is why all Police officers are provided with appropriate training in self-defence and the controlled use of force and are equipped accordingly, so as to protect their safety and that of others.

Opinions can differ on what is a reasonable amount of force, but one thing is certain - the person who is applying the force does not have the right to decide how much force it is reasonable to use. If it ends up in court, the person who applied the force would always believe he or she was acting reasonably and would never be guilty of any offence. It is for the jury, as ordinary members of the community, to decide the amount of force which it would be reasonable to use in the circumstances of each case. It is relevant that the person was under pressure from an imminent attack and might not have had time to make entirely rational decisions, so the test must balance the objective standard of a reasonable person by attributing some of the subjective knowledge of the defendant, including his or her beliefs as to the surrounding circumstances, even if mistaken. However, even allowing for any mistakes made in a crisis, the amount of force must be proportionate and reasonable given the value of the interests being protected and the harm likely to be caused by use of force. The classic test comes from the Jamaican case of Palmer v The Queen, on appeal to the Privy Council in 1971:

"The defence of self-defence is one which can be and will be readily understood by any jury. It is a straightforward conception. It involves no abstruse legal thought. ...Only common sense is needed for its understanding. It is both good law and good sense that a man who is attacked may defend himself. It is both good law and good sense that he may do, but may only do, what is reasonably necessary. But everything will depend upon the particular facts and circumstances. It may in some cases be only sensible and clearly possible to take some simple avoiding action.

Some attacks may be serious and dangerous. Others may not be. If there is some relatively minor attack it would not be common sense to permit some action of retaliation which was wholly out of proportion to the necessities of the situation.

If an attack is serious so that it puts someone in immediate peril then immediate defensive action may be necessary. If the moment is one of crisis for someone in imminent danger he may have (to) avert the danger by some instant reaction. If the attack is all over and no sort of peril remains then the employment of force may be by way of revenge or punishment or by way of paying off an old score or may be pure aggression.

There may no longer be any link with a necessity of defence... If a jury thought that in a moment of unexpected anguish a person attacked had only done what he honestly and instinctively thought was necessary that would be most potent evidence that only reasonable defensive action had been taken."

In R v Lindsay (2005) AER (D) 349 the defendant who picked up a sword in self-defence, when attacked in his home by three masked intruders armed with loaded handguns, killed one of them by slashing him repeatedly with that sword. The prosecution case was that, although he had initially acted in self-defence, he had then lost his self-control and demonstrated a clear intent to kill the armed intruder. In fact, the defendant was himself a low-level cannabis dealer who kept the sword available to defend himself against other drug dealers. The Court of Appeal confirmed an eight-year term of imprisonment. In a non-criminal context, it would not be expected that ordinary householders who "go too far" when defending themselves against armed intruders would receive such a long sentence.

Self-defence in English law is a complete defence to all levels of assault, and can't be used to mitigate liability, say, from murder to manslaughter where a Police officer acting in the course of their duty uses a greater degree of force than necessary for self-defence. Hence, self-defence is distinguishable from provocation, which only applies to mitigate what would otherwise have been murder to manslaughter (i.e. provocation is not a complete defence).

Due to the completeness of the defence, self-defence is interpreted in a relatively conservative way to avoid creating too generous a standard of justification. The more forgiving a defence, the greater the incentive for a cynical defendant to exploit it when planning the use of violence or in explaining matters after the event. Thus, although the juries in self-defence cases are entitled to take into account the physical characteristics of the defendant, that evidence has little probative value in deciding whether excessive force was actually used. The general common law principle is stated in Beckford v R (1988) 1 AC 130:

"A defendant is entitled to use reasonable force to protect himself, others for whom he is responsible and his property. It must be reasonable."

Conveying a Prisoner

Once an arrest has been made you have a duty of care for the prisoner and as such should endeavour to convey them in a safe manner. The use of handcuffs to the rear is always a recommendation, as you never know how a person may react later on to being arrested, especially if the person being arrested is being placed in the back of a car. A violent offender is best conveyed in a prison van, where possible, to reduce risks further. You should check that the cuffs are on correctly and not too tight. Once arrested, a prisoner should not smoke or use a mobile phone.

Once in custody the detainee is taken in front of the custody sergeant who can authorise detention based on the account you have given and what they have been arrested for. The detainee will need to empty all of their pockets and remove any belts, chains, shoelaces, or anything that it is deemed they could harm themselves with. This property needs to be recorded and booked into custody. Pay particular attention to money and record individual amounts of coins and notes. Get the detainee, where possible, to agree with the amount of money and the property booked in. All property will be given back on the detainee's release. Once all details have been taken you will either take the detainee to a cell or a custody officer will take them down for you. At this point, you are free to leave custody.

Suspect Interviews

Suspect interviews can seem quite complicated at first but with practice, you will become proficient although many officers still have a script as an aid memoire. You first interview will only be conducted after you have sat in on quite a few interviews and understand the procedure and how it is carried out. The actual interview is the suspect's chance to give their account of what has happened and to either agree or deny an allegation.

The interview has set guidelines which have to be followed; this includes the actual questions that are asked.

The interview should be conducted sitting down and as far as possible in comfort, with proper breaks for refreshment (normal meal breaks and at least 15 minutes every two hours). The interview should take place in an adequately heated, lit and ventilated room. Before the start of the interview, it is advisable to ensure that all persons present have switched off mobile telephones, pagers, etc to avoid interruptions. The suspect should be given the option to have legal representation and, if a minor, an appropriate adult present - a parent, guardian or an impartial Police designated appropriate adult (volunteer).

When there are grounds to suspect that a person has committed an offence, you must caution them before any questions about it are put to them, to ensure that the answers (or any failure to answer) are capable of being admissible in evidence in a prosecution. You should then put to them any significant statement(s) or silence(s) which occurred in your presence, or of any other interviewing officer, before the interview, and which have not been put before the suspect in a previous interview. You should ask the suspect whether they confirm or deny that earlier statement or silence and if they wish to add anything.

You must not try to obtain answers by the use of oppression. Such an approach is likely to mean that any evidence obtained is inadmissible.

You should also give the suspect the opportunity, where practicable, to read the record and sign it as correct, or to indicate the respects in which they consider it inaccurate. If the suspect agrees the record is correct, they should be asked to endorse the record with, for example, 'I agree this is a correct record of what was said' and add their signature. Where the suspect disagrees with the record, you should record the details of any disagreement and ask the suspect to read these details and sign them to the effect that they accurately reflect their disagreement. Any refusal to sign should also be recorded.

Tape Recorded Interview Guide

Persons Present

I am…. (State name rank and number). The date is…… The time is…….

This interview is being recorded at….(Police Station) and may be given in evidence if the case comes to trial.

I am interviewing……(suspect). Please state your full name, date of birth and address…..

Also present is my colleague……..(state name, Rank, and number if present).

If Solicitor is present - state your name and the firm you represent.

If an appropriate adult, interpreter, etc is present - Please state your name and relationship to the suspect.

There are no other persons present in this interview.

If a solicitor is not present - I must remind you that you are entitled to free and independent legal advice. You are entitled to this at any time during this interview. You may contact a solicitor by telephone and the interview can be delayed for you to obtain that advice. Do you understand?

Do you want a solicitor at this time?

Legal Advice

If the right to legal advice is waived - Ask why

If previously asked for legal advice and has now changed their mind - you previously said you wanted legal advice, I understand you have now changed your mind. Is this correct?

Caution

You do not have to say anything. But it may harm your defence if you do not mention when questioned something you later rely on in court. Anything you do say may be given in evidence.

Do you understand?

The reason for this interview is because you have been arrested on suspicion of (include "What. Where and When" for the offence).

Significant Statement/Silences

I wish to speak to you about the comments/silences made at the time of your arrest, prior to your arrival at the Police station, in addition to any other comments made prior to interview.

You said.......Do you agree this was said?

This is my opportunity to question you with regards to this matter. It is also your opportunity to give an explanation if you wish.

The wording of the Special Warning

I am investigating an offence of.......(state offence).

I want your account for.....(state fact/item).

I believe that......(state fact/item) may be due to you taking part in the commission of the offence.....(state offence).

I must inform you that a court may draw a proper inference if you fail or refuse to answer satisfactorily questions about (state fact/item).

That a record is being made of the interview and it may be given in evidence if you are brought to trial.

If previously stated 1) and 5) do not need to be repeated.

I have explained to you what may occur. Do you understand what I have said?

Explanation – It means that if you are reported/charged for the offence and you have failed to answer these questions, the magistrate or jury can ask themselves the question "Why didn't they explain when given the chance?" Whatever they consider the answer to be it can be taken into account when deciding guilt or innocence.

Closure

Do you wish to clarify anything?

Have you said all you wish to say about this matter?

The time is now......The date is........

Do you agree I am handing you a form explaining access to the tapes?

I am now stopping the recording.

Everything is done to set guidelines so that the crown prosecution service (CPS) can put a case before the court. That is unless a Police caution has been given by the custody sergeant, or a decision that there are no charges to answer has been made by the CPS.

Stop and Search

Stop and search is another common aspect of police work. You may be doing a stop check on a group of teenagers or a stop search on a person suspected to be carrying drugs. Stop and Search is so that Police officers are allowed to combat street crime and anti-social behaviour and to prevent more serious crimes.

You have to have grounds to stop somebody, even more so to actually search a person, and that is what we will go through in this section.

What is a stop? There are three different types of stops that you may utilise:

Stop - when a police officer or PCSO stops a person or persons in a public place and asks them to account for themselves. You may ask the following questions:

What are you doing?

Where have you been?

Where are you going?

What are you carrying?

Stop and Search - when a police officer stops and searches a person.

Vehicle - a police officer can stop any vehicle and ask the driver for driving documents. This is not the purpose of stop and search, but you can give documentation relevant to road traffic matters. It becomes a stop if:

The driver or any passengers are asked to account for themselves.

A search is carried out on the vehicle, driver or any passengers present.

The police officer or PCSO must explain why they are doing a stop and held to account for the stopped person's presence in an area.

There are plenty of occasions when you might talk to the public, and most of these do not qualify as either a 'stop' or 'stop and search'.

You have not officially 'stopped' someone if, for example:

You are asked for directions or information.

A person has witnessed a crime and is questioned about it to establish the background to the incident.

The person has been in an area where a crime recently occurred and is questioned about what they might have seen.

Here are some facts about stop and search:

The search has to take place on the street.

You can only ask someone to remove a hat, coat and gloves, or anything they wear for religious reasons. They must be taken somewhere out of public view for a search.

You can ask them to turn out their pockets and show you the contents of their bag.

You can also search their vehicle, even if they are not present, but you must leave a notice to say what you have done.

If they are carrying something illegal, such as a weapon, or you believe they have committed a crime, you may arrest them.

If you don't find anything, you must record details for monitoring purposes and they can request a copy of the stop check or stop search.

You need to ask the person stopped some basic details, which they don't have to give. These are name, address and date of birth. You will also ask them their ethnic origin so that the force can monitor disproportionate stopping of ethnic minorities and encourage Police accountability.

You will need to fill out a form outlining the reason for stopping the person, the outcome of the stop and search and your collar number and name, and give them a copy. This information will not be held on file unless the person stopped is charged with an offence.

Warrants

In England & Wales, arrest warrants can be issued for both suspects and witnesses. Arrest warrants for suspects can be issued by a justice of the peace under section 1 of the Magistrates' Courts act 1980 if information (in writing) is laid before them that a person has committed or is suspected of having committed an offence. Such arrest warrants can only be issued for someone over 18 if:

the offence to which the warrant relates is an indictable offence or is punishable with imprisonment, or

the person's address is not sufficiently established for a summons to be served on him.

Arrest warrants for witnesses can be issued if:

a justice of the peace is satisfied on oath that:

any person in England or Wales is likely to be able to give material evidence, or produce any document or thing likely to be material evidence, at the summary trial of an information by a magistrates' court,

it is in the interests of justice to issue a summons under this subsection to secure the attendance of that person to give evidence or produce the document or thing, and

it is probable that a summons would not procure the attendance of the person in question.

or, if:

a person has failed to attend court in response to a summons, the court is satisfied by evidence on oath that he is likely to be able to give material evidence or produce any document or thing likely to be material evidence in the proceedings

it is proved on oath, or in such other manner as may be prescribed, that he has been duly served with the summons, and that a reasonable sum has been paid or tendered to him for costs and expenses, and

it appears to the court that there is no just excuse for the failure.

Search Warrant

Search warrants are issued by a local magistrate and require a Constable to provide evidence to support the warrant application. In the vast majority of cases where the Police already hold someone in custody, searches of premises can be made without a search warrant under Section 18 of the Police and Criminal Evidence Act (PACE), which requires only the authority of a Police Inspector.

Searches under section 18 Police and Criminal Evidence Act can be conducted immediately by a Constable without the requirement for an Inspector's authorisation under section 18(5)a of PACE. This subsection allows a Constable to search the address of a suspect(s) under arrest in their presence before being presented to a Police station (or other custody suite).

If a person is arrested on their own property or just after leaving their premises, a Constable may immediately search both them and the immediate area where the person was under Section 32 of PACE.

Evidence Seizure and Crime Scene Preservation

The crime scene is a highly important source of physical evidence and is where forensic science investigations begin. From the point of collection to the time of archiving, evidence must be kept within a strict chain of custody to ensure no possible cross-contamination with any other objects. The methods employed to collect and preserve evidence are crucial and it is important that fundamental practices are adhered to.

Arrival at the crime scene

Upon arrival at the scene of the crime, the first officer must record the time, date and weather conditions and take action to preserve and secure the area to the maximum extent possible. This may involve putting a cordon in place to prevent any further contamination of the crime scene.

The administering of medical assistance to victims on the crime scene takes priority although any unauthorised access must minimal and were possible disallowed as any individual present poses the risk of contaminating or destroying physical evidence.

Once the scene has been secured, the investigating officer must evaluate the scene and decide on the system for examination to be employed by the crime-scene investigators. Immediate action must be taken to protect items of evidence, which may be destroyed by weather conditions or fire etc. Any persons present at the scene of the crime who may be witnesses should be removed and their details taken. It is also necessary to record all movements at the scene and any items moved or touched by individuals.

Recording at the crime scene

Recording the scene in its original state is highly important both as an aid for the subsequent investigation and also as evidence in court when the details of the crime scene and location of physical evidence must be provided. Various methods of recording the crime scene can include photography, sketches and written notes. Thorough in most instances recording usually requires that all three methods be employed.

The crime scene will firstly be photographed as thoroughly as possible and from various angles; suspected entrances and exits, any surrounding areas or areas where events in relation to the crime occurred should be included. Items of physical evidence should be photographed to show their position and location relative to the scene. Close-up photographs should then be taken to show the evidence in as greater detail as possible and alongside a measuring scale to ascertain size. If a body is present at the crime scene, this also should be photographed from various angles to show all injuries and weapons; the surface beneath the body is then be photographed upon its removal.

Rough sketches are made at the crime scene to give an accurate portrayal of the scene including dimensions and the location of items of physical evidence in relation to each other. The locations of approaches such as roadways, paths, entrances, exits and windows should be depicted. The size and dimensions of the area or building should be measured, with all measurements being made with a tape measure and the compass direction of north should be indicated. The exact locations of objects are determined by distance measurements from two fixed points, for example the walls of a room. Generally, objects are indicated by the assignment of letters, which are then referred to below the sketch with a description of the item. The initial sketch is usually a rough one, used to give maximum information but without care and attention to appearance. This sketch is then used to prepare a finished sketch, usually carried out by a skilled worker, which is drawn to scale and includes details of the articles of evidence.

Alongside both the sketches and photographs, note taking will play an important role throughout the processing of the crime scene. A detailed written description of the scene and physical evidence should be included, along with the times of discovery and the individuals coming in contact with the evidence. Tape-recording notes can often be more beneficial as it is a much quicker method of note taking, but this must later be transcribed into a written document for use as evidence.

Searching the crime scene for evidence

A systematic search of the crime scene is highly important so that no evidence is left unrecorded and for maximum information to be obtained; the more evidence gathered, the stronger the case. The investigator in charge of the crime-scene generally co-ordinates the search for evidence to ensure that all necessary areas are covered but also to ensure there is no duplication of effort. A forensic scientist is not usually present at the scene of a crime, unless the evidence is very involved. Trained field evidence technicians who are skilled in photography and examination, are sometimes employed to locate and collect physical evidence. The choice of search method is that of the evidence collectors and usually depends on the size and type of the crime scene and on the number of individuals participating. Search methods include the spiral search method, in which the collection of evidence is carried out in a circular pattern working towards a fixed point at the centre; the grid method in which the area is searched along horizontal and vertical lines of a grid; a strip or line search; and the quadrant method where the area is divided into segments for individual searching. Experiences of the investigating officer and the type of crime committed will generally determine the search method employed.

While searching the crime scene, any doubted item should be treated as evidence until it can be proven otherwise. Gloves and protective clothing should be worn to prevent contamination of the scene. Along with collecting evidence, it is also important to collect known standards, for example, fibre samples from carpets and furnishings. For any material stained with biological fluids collected for analysis, a clean piece of the same material should be collected separately as a control.

Maintaining the chain of custody

The chain of custody of an evidential item begins at the initial collection of the evidence at the scene of crime and must be presented if the evidence is used in court. The authenticity and integrity of the evidence relies upon the detailed recorded history of the item, including the persons who came into possession of the item and the examination tests performed upon it. Establishing set guidelines on recording and labelling of the history of the evidence during its time retained by the police is the most effective way to ensure this of custody is maintained. You may find yourself being asked to take part in a search of a house using a warrant or to search an area following a crime. You may even find an item whilst out on patrol.

In all cases you need to make a record of what you have found and the location it was found. An item found on the street on patrol will often just be recorded in a lost property book or something similar, but it must be recorded.

If the item found is linked to a crime then it needs to be recorded as a seized exhibit, with a seizure statement being.

Always consider carefully the evidence that may need to be collected.

When taking items into possession, seek, whenever possible, to obtain the best evidence available.

Consider proportionality, and issues of evidential significance.

Record in your notebook all objects (including evidential documents) taken.

Consideration needs to be given to the type of bag or container the exhibit needs to be placed in.

Packaging

Physical evidence must then be properly packaged and labelled, with different samples requiring different methods of packaging. For example, while hairs and fibres can be contained within plastic containers, any items containing biological evidence such as blood or semen must be air-dried before packaging and placed in paper bags to remove the problem of moisture build-up and contamination from bacterial growth.

Packages should be labelled with the time and date of packaging, the name of the packager and any history of any known contact with the evidence. Where possible, the actual item of evidence should be labelled for identification, in addition to labelling the packaging in which it is placed.

Any items apart from clothes - place each item into a separate plastic police evidence bag. Package firearms and ammunition separately; seek individual force advice. Knives can be placed into a special knife container.

Clothing - empty pockets. Place each item of clothing into a separate paper police evidence bag (but put any wet/blood soaked item inside an open plastic police evidence bag first).

Hold seal away from your face and expel air from bag; close bag by folding top twice.

Sign two signature seals and place over fold.

Wrap 2-inch sellotape around fold to form an airtight seal. Any potential for leakage must be eliminated - especially at the corners; go right to the edge of the bag.

Fold bottom of bag once (or twice if your model has blue tabs).

Complete and affix a label.

Finally (in case the label might come off) write exhibit number, date, taken by, description of exhibit and exhibit name directly onto the bag.

PACE
The Police and Criminal Evidence Act (PACE) and the PACE Codes of Practice provide the core framework of Police powers and safeguards around stop and search, arrest, detention, investigation, identification and interviewing detainees.

Code A deals with the exercise by police officers of statutory powers to search a person or a vehicle without first making an arrest. It also deals with the need for a Police officer to make a record of a stop or encounter.

Code B deals with Police powers to search premises and to seize and retain property found on premises and persons.

Code C sets out the requirements for the detention, treatment and questioning of suspects, not related to terrorism, in police custody by Police officers.

Code D concerns the main methods used by the police to identify people in connection with the investigation of offences and the keeping of accurate and reliable criminal records.

Code E deals with the audio recording of interviews with suspects in the police station.

Code F deals with the visual recording with sound of interviews with suspects. There is no statutory requirement for police officers to visually record interviews. However, the contents of this code should be considered if an interviewing officer decides to make a visual recording with sound of an interview with a suspect.

Code G deals with powers of arrest under section 24 the Police and Criminal Evidence Act 1984 as amended by section 110 of the Serious Organised Crime and Police Act 2005.

Code H sets out the requirements for the detention, treatment and questioning of suspects related to terrorism in Police custody by Police officers.

RTC

RTC (Road Traffic Collision) can be anything from a minor bump up to a major accident that involves fatalities. Any RTC will usually start with making sure everyone is ok and if first on scene alerting any other emergency services that may be required. With any injured persons dealt with the next priority will be the traffic and deciding if any form of traffic management is required or the road needs to be closed. Most simple bumps or shunts can be dealt with quite simply and often disruption to other traffic is minimal. But you need to be aware of your own safety as well as those involved in the RTC. Especially if the RTC occurred on a fast or busy main road. Consider if the traffic needs to be stopped or re-directed.

As soon as you get called to an accident were there is either life changing injuries or a fatality the scene of the accident becomes a crime scene and as such will require the road closing and a cordon putting in place. So that an accident investigator can assess the scene and collect vital evidence in order to ascertain what has happened.

Any RTC usually requires some form of accident card being completed. Most are a simple tick sheet with an area to draw a diagram of the RTC. If there are injuries these will also need to be recorded. As a rule of thumb from anyone involved in the RTC make sure you take:

Name, Address, Date of Birth and a contact number along with the vehicle registration. The vehicle and drivers details should be checked at the scene and any drivers involved needs to be breathalyzed were possible. If taken to hospital and a more serious RTC then a blood sample would have to be obtained for testing.

Conflict Resolution

Conflict resolution is a range of processes aimed at alleviating or eliminating sources of conflict. As a police officer, many of the incidents you may attend will require conflict resolution, so what is it? The term "conflict resolution" is sometimes used interchangeably with the terms "dispute resolution" or "alternative dispute resolution". Processes of conflict resolution generally include negotiation, mediation and diplomacy.

Talking at the right level without aggression can often calm people down. Once you have stepped up a level of aggression it is nearly impossible to step down. People will often respond well to being spoken to in a quiet and polite manner even if they have a very aggressive demeanour themselves. Stay calm listen and reply in a positive manner

There are many tools available to persons in conflict. One option would be not to fight over it, no violence, only talking out the problem. How and when they are used depends on several factors (such as the specific issues at stake in the conflict). Sometimes taking away a person or persons, either through arrest or simply a distance apart could help. That could be down the street, or into another room to talk through what has happened and help calm the situation down. The tools you can use to aid conflict resolution include negotiation, advocacy, diplomacy, activism, nonviolence and critical pedagogy: you can also utilise outside agencies who can arrange or use a community building, mediation and counselling for a longer term resolution.

Victim Care

Victim care may seem like something simple but it is all too easy to overlook. A victim of a crime is looking to you to investigate and, if possible, solve the crime. It may be the first time that person has spoken to, or needed, the Police. Try to treat a victim the same way you would treat a member of your family. Spend time reassuring and explaining what you can do. If further investigation is needed, then keep them updated with what is happening. All victims, or indeed anyone who comes into contact with the Police, deserve a positive experience and should be treated fairly and with empathy and understanding. Never give false hopes or promises and never feel embarrassed to say "I will find out and get back to you", but make sure you do get back to them. In the end the public are our customers and more and more the word customer care is banded about in police force training.

As mentioned in the radio section, "managing expectation's" is another key term. Everyone has expectations of what they expect to happen or to be done. Sometimes the expectations are not part of the police remit. For example civil matters or when you have not turned up as quickly as the victim would have expected. It is important to remain polite and fully explain what you are able to do as well as what you are unable to do.

This all sounds basic but it is all too easy to forget when you want to make an arrest or resolve an incident quickly if there are several other jobs coming in.

Human Rights

The Human Rights Act 1998 gives further legal effect in the UK to the fundamental rights and freedoms contained in the ECHR. These rights not only impact matters of life and death, they also affect the rights you have in your everyday life: what you can say and do, your beliefs, your right to a fair trial and other similar basic entitlements.

Most rights have limits to ensure that they do not unfairly damage other people's rights. However, certain rights – such as the right not to be tortured – can never be limited by a court or anybody else.

If any of these rights and freedoms are breached, you have a right to an effective solution in law, even if the breach was by someone in authority, such as a Police officer. This means that as a Police officer it is important to be aware of the Human Rights Act and know how a detainee for example should be treated.

Article 2: Right to Life

(1) Everyone's right to life shall be protected by law. No one shall be deprived of his life intentionally save in the execution of a sentence of a court following his conviction of a crime for which the penalty is provided by law.
(2) Deprivation of life shall not be regarded as inflicted in contravention of this article when it results from the use of force which is no more than absolutely necessary- (a) in defence of any person from unlawful violence;
(b) in order to effect a lawful arrest or to prevent the escape of a person lawfully detained;
(c) in action lawfully taken for the purpose of quelling a riot or insurrection.

Article 3: Inhuman treatment

No one shall be subjected to torture or to inhuman or degrading treatment or punishment.

Article 4: Slavery

(1) No one shall be held in slavery or servitude.
(2) No one shall be required to perform forced or compulsory

labour.

(3) For the purpose of this article the term "forced or compulsory labour" shall not include:

(a) any work required to be done in the ordinary course of detention imposed in accordance to the provisions of article 5 of this convention or during conditional release from such detention;

(b) any service of a military character or, in the case of conscientious objectors in countries where they are recognised, service exacted instead of compulsory military service;

(c) any service exacted in case of an emergency or calamity threatening the life or well-being of the community;

(d) any work or service which forms part of normal civic obligations.

Article 5: Right to Liberty

(1) Everyone has the right to liberty and security of person. No one shall be deprived of his liberty save in the following cases and in accordance with a procedure prescribed by law:

(a) the lawful detention of a person after conviction by a competent court;

(b) the lawful arrest or detention of a person for non-compliance with the lawful order of a court or in order to secure the fulfillment of any obligation prescribed by law;

(c) the lawful arrest or detention of a person effected for the purpose of bringing him before the competent legal authority on reasonable suspicion of having committed an offence or when it is reasonably considered necessary to prevent his committing an offence or fleeing after having done so;

(d) the detention of a minor by lawful order for the purpose of educational supervision or his lawful detention for the purpose of bringing him before the competent legal authority;

(e) the lawful detention of persons for the prevention of the spreading of infectious diseases, of persons of unsound mind, alcoholics and drug addicts or vagrants;

(f) the lawful arrest or detention of a person to prevent his effecting an unauthorised entry into the country or of a person against whom action is being taken with a view to deportation or extradition.

(2) Everyone who is arrested shall be informed promptly, in a language which he understands, of the reason for his arrest and of any charge against him.

(3) Everyone arrested or detained in accordance with the provisions of paragraph 1(c) of this article shall be brought promptly before a judge or other officer authorised by law to exercise judicial power and shall be entitled to trial within a reasonable time or to release pending trial. Release may be conditioned by guarantees to appear for trial.

(4) Everyone who is deprived of his liberty by arrest or detention shall be entitled to take proceedings by which the lawfulness of his detention shall be decided speedily by a court and his release ordered if the detention is not lawful.

(5) Everyone who has been the victim of arrest or detention in contravention of the provisions of this article shall have an enforceable right to compensation.

Article 6: Right to a fair trial

(1) In the determination of his civil rights and obligations or of any criminal charge against him, everyone is entitled to a fair and public hearing within a reasonable time by an independent and impartial tribunal established by law. Judgment shall be pronounced publicly but the press and public may be excluded from all or part of the trial in the interests of morals, public order or national security in a democratic society, where the interests of juveniles or the protection of the private life of the parties so require, or to the extent strictly necessary in the

opinion of the court in special circumstances where publicity would prejudice the interests of justice.

(2) Everyone charged with a criminal offence shall be presumed innocent until proved guilty according to law.

(3) Everyone charged with a criminal offence has the following minimum rights -

(a) to be informed promptly, in a language which he understands and in detail, of the nature and cause of the accusation against him;

(b) to have adequate time and facilities for the preparation of his defence;

(c) to defend himself in person or through legal assistance of his own choosing or, if he has not sufficient means to pay for legal assistance, to be given it free when the interests of justice so require;

(d) to examine or have examined witnesses against him and to obtain the attendance and examination of witnesses on his behalf under the same conditions as witnesses against him;

(e) to have the free assistance of an interpreter if he cannot understand or speak the language used in court.

Article 7: Retrospective crimes

(1) No one shall be held guilty of any criminal offence on account of any Act or omission which did not constitute a criminal offence under national or international law at the time when it was committed. Nor shall a heavier penalty be imposed than the one that was applicable at the time the criminal offence was committed.

(2) This article shall not prejudice the trial and punishment of any person for any Act or omission which, at the time it was committed, was criminal according to the general law recognised by civilised nations.

Article 8: Right to privacy

(1) Everyone has the right for his private and family life, his home and his correspondence.

(2) There shall be no interference by a public authority with the exercise of this right except such as is in accordance with the law and is necessary in a democratic society in the interests of national security, public safety or the economic well-being of the country, for the prevention of disorder or crime, for the protection of health or morals, or for the protection of the rights and freedoms of others.

Article 9: Freedom of conscience

(1) Everyone has the right to freedom of thought, conscience and religion; this right includes freedom to change his religion or belief and freedom, either alone or in community with others and in public or private, to manifest his religion or belief, in worship, teaching, practice and observance.

(2) Freedom to manifest one's religion or beliefs shall be subject only to such limitations as are prescribed by law and are necessary in a democratic society in the interests of public safety, for the protection of public order, health or morals, or for the protection of the rights and freedoms of others.

Article 10: Freedom of Expression

(1) Everyone has the right of freedom of expression. This right shall include freedom to hold opinions and to receive and impart information and ideas without inference by public authority and regardless of frontiers. This article shall not prevent states from requiring the licensing of broadcasting, television or cinema enterprises.

(2) The exercise of these freedoms, since it carries with it duties and responsibilities, may be subject to such formalities, conditions, restrictions or penalties as are prescribed by law and

are necessary in a democratic society, in the interests of national security, territorial integrity or public safety, for the prevention of disorder or crime, for the protection of health or morals, for the protection of the reputation or rights of others, for preventing the disclosure of information received in confidence, or for maintaining the authority and impartiality of the judiciary.

Article 11: Freedom of Assembly

(1) Everyone has the right to freedom of peaceful assembly and to freedom of association with others, including the right to form and to join trade unions for the protection of his interests.

(2) No restrictions shall be placed on the exercise of these rights other than such as are prescribed by law and are necessary in a democratic society in the interests of national security or public safety, for the prevention of disorder or crime, for the protection of health or morals or for the protection of the rights and freedoms of others.

This article shall not prevent the imposition of lawful restrictions on the exercise of these rights by members of the armed forces, of the Police or of the administration of the state.

Article 12: Marriage and the family

Men and women of marriageable age shall have the right to marry and to found a family, according to national laws governing the exercise of this right.

Article 14: Discrimination

The enjoyment of the rights and freedoms set forth in this convention shall be secured without discrimination on any ground such as sex, race, colour, language, religion, political or other opinion, national or social origin, association with a national minority, property, birth or other status.

Protocol No 1

Article 1

Every natural or legal person is entitled to the peaceful enjoyment of his possessions. No one shall be deprived of his possessions except in the public interest and subject to the conditions provided for by law and by the general principles of international law.

The preceding provisions shall not, however, in any way impair the right of the state to enforce such laws as it deems necessary to control the use of property in accordance with the general interest or to secure payment of taxes or other contributions or penalties.

Article 2

No person shall be denied a right to an education. In the exercise of any functions which it assumes in relation to education and to teaching, the state shall respect the right of parents to ensure such education and teaching in conformity with their own religious and philosophical convictions.

Article 3

The High Contracting Parties undertake to hold free elections at reasonable intervals by secret ballot, under conditions which will ensure the free expression of the opinion of the people in the choice of the legislature.

LAW AND OFFENCES

What is the law and what laws do I need to know? What is crime and what do I do if I see a crime and what crime can I arrest for?

The law in itself is a wide subject so we will look at the law and crimes that you would typically come across on the beat as a police officer.

We will start by asking what is the law?

The easiest way is to give the definition of law from the English dictionary

"– Binding or enforceable rule: a rule of conduct or procedure recognised by a community as binding or enforceable by authority - piece of legislation: an Act passed by a Parliament or similar body - legal system: the body or system of rules recognised by a community that are enforceable by established process."

As a Police officer it is your duty to uphold the law and gather evidence. You do not make the direct decision to prosecute or bring the case to court; that is the job of the CPS.

From this we can see that a law is something we all abide by and should not break in our day to day lives. Law itself is broken down into different types of law; ones you will come across are common law, criminal law, and civil law.

Common Law

The definition - this is evolved law - the body of law developed as a result of custom and judicial decisions, as distinct from the law laid down by legislative assemblies - and forms the basis of all law that is applied.

Criminal Law

The definition - the branch of law dealing with crime: it defines the nature of crimes and sets suitable punishments for them.

Civil Law

The definition - law of citizens' rights: the law of a state dealing with the rights of private citizens.

English law is the legal system of England and Wales. It was exported to Commonwealth countries while the British Empire was established and maintained, and it forms the basis of the jurisprudence of most of those countries. English law prior to the American Revolution is still part of the law of the United states through reception statutes, except in Louisiana, and provides the basis for many American legal traditions and policies, though it has no superseding jurisdiction.

English law in its strictest sense applies within the jurisdiction of England and Wales. Any legislation which the Welsh Assembly enacts is enacted in particular circumscribed policy areas defined by the Government of Wales Act 2006, other legislation of the UK Parliament, or by orders in council given under the authority of the 2006 act. Furthermore, that legislation is, as with any by law made by any other body within England and Wales, interpreted by the undivided judiciary of England and Wales.

Scottish law is a unique legal system with an ancient basis in Roman law. Grounded in uncodified civil law dating back to the

Corpus Juris Civilis (Roman Body of Civil Law), it also features elements of common law with medieval sources. This means Scotland has a pluralistic, or mixed legal system. South Africa has a similar system to Scotland.

Since the Acts of Union, in 1707, it has shared a legislature with the rest of the United Kingdom. Before 1707 Scotland retained a fundamentally different legal system from that of England and Wales, but the Union brought English influence on Scots law. In recent years, Scots law has also been affected by European law under the Treaty of Rome, the requirements of the ECHR (entered into by members of the Council of Europe) and the establishment of the Scottish Parliament, which may pass legislation within its areas of legislative competence as detailed by the Scotland act 1998.

There are substantial differences between Scottish and English law. Some of the more important practical differences between the jurisdictions include; the age of legal capacity (16 years old in Scotland, 18 years old in England); the use of a 15 member jury in Scotland rather than the usual 12 members; the fact that the accused in a criminal trial does not have the right to elect a judge or jury trial; judges and juries of criminal trials have the "third verdict" of "not proven" available to them, and the fact that Equity does not exist in Scots law. Some of the more important practical similarities between the jurisdictions include the similar protections for consumers under the Sale of Goods Act 1979, very similar treatment under various taxation legislation and similar protections for employees and agents.

Criminal Law - criminal acts are considered offences against the whole of a community or the state in addition to certain international organisations. All have responsibility for crime prevention and for bringing the culprits to justice as well as dealing with the convicted offenders. The Police, the criminal courts and prisons are all publicly funded services, though the main focus of criminal law concerns the role of the courts, how they apply criminal statutes passed by legislatures as well as common law, and why they criminalise some forms of behaviour.

The fundamentals of a crime are known as the actus reus and the mens rea of the crime. These two Latin terms mean "guilty Act" (doing that which is prohibited) and "guilty mind" (i.e. the intent to commit the crime). The traditional view is that moral culpability requires that you should have recognised or intended that you were acting wrongly. Nevertheless, most jurisdictions have many strict liability offences, which criminalise behaviour without the need to show moral wrongdoing. These are usually regulatory in nature, where the result of breach could have particularly harmful results, for instance, drink driving, but are sometimes purely paternalistic, as in charges of statutory rape for consensual sex. Offences can range from ones resulting in fatality, such as murder and manslaughter, to non-deadly offences against people, such as ABH or grievous bodily harm (GBH), to offences concerning people's property, like criminal damage, theft, robbery or burglary.

Importantly, you can still be liable for helping another person's criminal Act - aiding and abetting an offender or conspiring to do something prohibited, or merely attempting to commit an offence, like attempted criminal damage. Defences exist to some crimes, so that in some jurisdictions a person who is accused can plead they are insane and did not understand what they were doing, that they were not in control of their bodies, they were intoxicated, mistaken about what they were doing, acted in self-defence, acted under duress or out of necessity, or were provoked. These are issues to be raised at trial and form part of the defence for the accused, for which there are detailed rules of evidence and procedure to be followed. As a Police officer it is your role to gather all the facts and evidence, investigate the crime and prove the intent so that the CPS can see if there is a case to be proven at court. We shall look at evidence and its importance later on in the chapter.

Common Law - the essence of English common law is that it is made by judges sitting in courts, applying their common sense and knowledge of legal precedent (stare decisis) to the facts before them. A decision of the highest appeal court in England and Wales, the House of Lords, is binding on every other court in the hierarchy, and they will follow its directions. England and Wales are constituent countries of the United Kingdom, which is a member of the European Union. Hence, EU law is a part of English law. The European Union consists mainly of countries that use civil law and so the civil law system is also in England in this form. The European Court of Justice can direct English and Welsh courts on the meaning of areas of law in which the EU has passed legislation.

The oldest law currently in force is the Distress act 1267, part of the Statute of Marlborough, (52 Hen. 3). Three sections of the Magna Carta, originally signed in 1215 and a landmark in the development of English law, are extant, but they date to the reissuing of the law in 1297.

Apart from a very few examples of local custom and tradition that survive in England's legal system, law that is not contained within a specific act is known as common law. It is built up by the courts and their judgments. This means that, in deciding a particular case, the court must have regard to the principles of law laid down in earlier reported cases on the same or similar points, although the law may be extended or varied if the facts of the particular case are sufficiently different.

In fact, many aspects of the law shown here are also controlled by statute law (which is the law made by Parliament) but as a general heading, these matters can be grouped together as based on, or originating in, common law.

There are several examples relevant to the countryside and used by rangers and others who are required to enforce laws and bye-laws.

Scottish common law is often different from English, and sometimes significantly so. The following examples apply to English law.

Trespass - as applied to a piece of land open to the public which is not common land, open access land, or a public right of way. This is one of the areas where the laws of England and Scotland are significantly different. It is against the law to trespass on any land (and inland that includes land covered by water such as rivers or lakes) or in any building. Ignorance of that fact is no defence under this law. The word trespass covers much more than people usually realise. All land in this country belongs to someone. If you go on to land without he owner's permission, you are trespassing unless there is some right of access for the public, or for you specifically (for example if you have acquired a right to pass over the land to reach some land of your own).

Any person can enter a place if the landowner permits it. However, this does not necessarily make a permanent right of access, and unless they have dedicated a bit of land to be permanently open it is within the power of the landowner to ask any person to leave, assuming that person does not have some other lawful reason to be there. The landowner does not have to give a reason. If the person does not go immediately, by the shortest practical route, then they are trespassing. Despite the well-known sign 'trespassers will be prosecuted', trespass is not a criminal offence and trespassers cannot usually be prosecuted. They can, however, be sued. There is little chance of such a matter ever being so serious as to be worth suing over, and so this rarely happens.

People in a park will often protest (if asked to leave) that it is public land. However, the ownership of the land is not relevant. Even if the land is owned by a public body, such as the local council, this does not mean necessarily that they have a right to be on it at all times - they do not. If the place closes at a certain time and a visitor remains after that time, they can then be considered to be trespassing. If a visitor misbehaves at any time and refuses to leave when asked to do so by someone with a right to do so (usually the landowner or a representative), then the visitor could become a trespasser because they no longer have the landowner's permission to be there, even if they entered legally. Note: this also gives landowners the absolute right to close off paths (other than rights of way) and areas without notice or explanation. You may well come across a lot of trespassing by young people using parks after closing time. This is often just for a social meeting but it can also be to consume alcohol or to take drugs.

This law is of little practical use but might be employed when arguing with more reasonable people. It does not apply to people on a public footpath or other right of way, or on open access land. The problem is that if someone is trespassing, they are unlikely to comply with a polite request to leave, and if they do not, the landowner has little, if any, further recourse. Section 61 of the Criminal Justice and Public Order Act 1994 allows the senior Police officer attending the scene of an incident involving a trespass or nuisance on land to order trespassers to leave the land and to remove their vehicles as soon as reasonably practicable. The power can only be used when there are two or more people there and they "are present there with the common purpose of residing there for any period, (and) that reasonable steps have been taken by or on behalf of the occupier to ask them to leave" and either the trespassers have six or more vehicles between them, or they have caused damage to the land or to property on the land or used threatening, abusive or insulting words or behaviour - or both. So really it's not likely to cover anything other than a major invasion. This power is not often used, but for practical purposes this is the only instance where you might get the Police to come and actually remove trespassers.

Sometimes, people go onto private property, which is not apparently fenced off and where the owners do not seem to mind. The fact that there is no fence or any sign saying that the land is private does not mean that people can go there. Wandering on to farmers' fields or other places which are obviously private is clearly trespassing. So is wandering over land which may not be so clearly private, if the public has no right of access.

It is not normally possible to be a trespasser whilst legitimately on a right of way. However, if the user is not using the right of way as a route to get from one place to another, but using it for some other reason, such as to interfere with the landowner, they can be considered to be a trespasser. A real example of this (before open access land was in existence) concerned a hunt saboteur who was deemed by a court to be a trespasser for shouting and waving flags, whilst on a footpath, on a grouse moor. This important distinction was the purpose for which the person was there. This does not mean that it is always wrong to shout and wave flags on a footpath.

Murder comes under common law as there is no statute making murder illegal. It is a common law crime - so although there is no written Act of Parliament making murder illegal, it is illegal by virtue of the constitutional authority of the courts and their previous decisions. Common law can be amended or repealed by Parliament; murder, by way of example, carries a mandatory life sentence today, but had previously allowed the death penalty.

Crime and Offences
Crime - for the final part of this chapter we shall look at what a crime is and go through some examples of crime that you may come across.
Society defines crime as the breach of one or more rules or laws for which some governing authority or force may ultimately prescribe a punishment.

Authorities employ various mechanisms to regulate behaviour, including rules codified into laws, policing people to ensure they comply with those laws and other policies and practices designed by the Police, government or local authorities to prevent crime. In addition, authorities try to provide remedies and sanctions, and collectively these constitute a criminal justice system. Not all breaches of the law, however, are considered crimes, for example, breaches of contract and other civil law offences.

Offence definition - legal or moral crime: an official crime or a crime against moral, social, or other accepted standards; anger or resentment: anger, resentment, hurt, or displeasure, cause of displeasure or anger. Something that causes displeasure, humiliation, anger, resentment, or hurt.

Below is a basic list of some of the more common crimes and offences you may come across whilst on duty.

We have two types of offences: Summary and Indictable offences.

Summary offence - this type of offence means offences like public disorder or anti-social behaviour and drunkenness, as well as most road traffic offences such as careless driving or speeding. Summary offences need to be tried in the magistrate's court. The magistrate's court has the powers to fine or send to prison. 90% of offences are heard in a magistrate's court.

Indictable offence – are so called because they are tried on indictment in the crown court by a judge and jury. They are offences that are more serious in nature, such as rape, robbery and murder.

Here are some common offences you may come across whilst on duty.

Malicious Communication
A person is guilty of malicious communications if they send to another person any form of communication of any description

which coveys a message of indecent or grossly offensive, threatening, information which is false or unknown or believed to be false by the sender. For the purpose to cause distress or anxiety to the intended person of the communication.
The defence is that the threat was used to reinforce a demand on reasonable grounds and that it was believed on reasonable grounds that the use of the threat was a proper means of reinforcing the demand.

Racist or Racially Aggravated
A racist or racially motivated offence that has been based on a victim having received verbal or physical hostility based upon race or religion.

Generally a racist or racially aggravated offence is when:

At the time of committing the offence or immediately before or after the offence, the person demonstrates towards the victim hostility based on a victim's membership of a racial or religious group, sexual orientation or gender,

The offence is motivated by hostility towards members of a racial or religious group based on their membership of that group.

Public Order
Public Order comes in different sections outlined below but as an overview it is to deal with public disorder or violence. It is dealt with under the 1986 Public Order Act, which replaced the common law and Public Order act of 1936.

Section 1 – Riot

(1) Where 12 or more persons who are present together use or threaten unlawful violence for a common purpose and the conduct of them (taken together) is such as would cause a person of reasonable firmness present at the scene to fear for his personal safety, each of the persons using unlawful violence for the common purpose is guilty of riot.

(2) It is immaterial whether or not the 12 or more use or threaten unlawful violence simultaneously.

(3) The common purpose may be inferred from conduct.

(4) No person of reasonable firmness need actually be, or be likely to be, present at the scene.

(5) Riot may be committed in private as well as in public places.

(6) A person guilty of riot is liable on conviction on indictment to imprisonment for a term not exceeding 10 years or a fine, or both.

Section 2 - Violent Disorder

(1) Where three or more persons who are present together use or threaten unlawful violence and the conduct of them (taken together) is such as would cause a person of reasonable firmness present at the scene to fear for his personal safety, each of the persons using or threatening unlawful violence is guilty of violent disorder.

(2) It is immaterial whether or not the three or more use or threaten unlawful violence simultaneously.

(3) Same as section 1.

(4) Same as section 1.

(5) A person guilty of violent disorder is liable on conviction on indictment to imprisonment for a term not exceeding five years or a fine, or both, or on summary conviction to imprisonment for a term not exceeding six months or a fine not exceeding the statutory maximum or both.

Section 3 - Affray

(1) A person is guilty of affray if he uses or threatens unlawful violence towards another and his conduct is such as would cause a person of reasonable firmness present at the scene to fear for his personal safety.

(2) Where two or more persons use or threaten unlawful violence, it is the conduct of them taken together that must be considered for the purposes of subsection (1).

(3) For the purposes of this section words cannot be made by the use of words alone.

(4) Same as section 1.

(5) Same as section 1.

(6) A Constable may arrest without warrant anyone he reasonably suspects is committing affray.

(7) A person guilty of affray is liable on conviction on indictment to imprisonment for a term not exceeding three years or a fine or both, or on summary conviction to imprisonment

for a term not exceeding six months or a fine not exceeding the statutory maximum or both.

Section 4 - Fear or provocation of violence

(1) A person is guilty of an offence if he - a) uses towards another person threatening, abusive or insulting words or behaviour, or b) distributes or displays to another person any writing, sign or other visible representation which is threatening, abusive or insulting, with intent to cause that person to believe that immediate unlawful violence will be used against him or another by any person, or to provoke the immediate use of unlawful violence by that person or another, or whereby that person is likely to believe that such violence will be provoked.

(2) An offence under this section may be committed in a public or a private place, except that no offence is committed where the words or behaviour are used, or the writing, sign or other visible representation is distributed or displayed, by a person inside a dwelling and the other person is also inside that or another dwelling.

(3) A Constable may arrest without warrant anyone he reasonably suspects is committing an offence under this subsection.

(4) A person guilty of an offence under this section is liable on summary conviction to imprisonment for a term not exceeding six months or a fine not exceeding level 5 (currently £5,000) on the standard scale or both.

Section 5 - Harassment, alarm or distress

(1) A person is guilty of an offence if he - a) uses threatening, abusive or insulting words or behaviour, or disorderly behaviour, or b) displays any writing, sign or other visible representation which is threatening, abusive or insulting, within the hearing or sight of a person likely to be causing harassment, alarm or distress thereby.

(2) An offence under this section may be committed in a public or a private place, except that no offence is committed where the words or behaviour are used, or the writing, sign or other visible representation is displayed, by a person inside a dwelling and the other person is also inside that or another dwelling.

(3) It is a defence for the accused to prove - a) that he had no reason to believe that there was any person within hearing or sight who was likely to be caused harassment, alarm or distress, or b) that he was inside a dwelling and had no reason to believe that the words or behaviour used, or the writing, sign or other visible representation displayed, would be heard or seen by a person outside that or any other dwelling, or c) that his conduct was reasonable.

(4) A Constable may arrest without warrant if - a) he engages in offensive conduct which the Constable warns him to stop, and b) he engages in further offensive conduct immediately or shortly after the warning.

(5) In subsection (4) above 'offensive conduct' means conduct the Constable reasonably suspects to constitute an offence under this section, and the conduct mentioned in paragraph (a) and the further conduct need not be of the same nature.

(6) A person guilty of an offence under this section is liable on summary conviction to a fine not exceeding level 3 (currently £1,000) on the standard scale.

Breach of the Peace

Constables are permitted to arrest a person to "prevent a further breach of the peace" which allows Police Constables to arrest a person before a breach of the peace has occurred. This is permitted when a Constable holds a reasonable belief that should the person remain, that they would continue with their course of conduct and that a breach of the peace would occur. Arrest for breach of the peace is usually used to remove violent or potentially violent offenders from a scene rapidly. The only punishment that can be inflicted by a court for this offence is for the offender to be bound over to keep the peace.

Offensive Weapon

"Any person who without lawful authority or reasonable excuse, the proof whereof shall lie on him, has with him in any public place any offensive weapon shall be guilty of an offence."
Punishable on summary conviction by three months' imprisonment or level 5 fine; on indictment by two years' imprisonment and/or maximum fine.

Although there is no express power of arrest for this offence, an arrest can be carried out if the general arrest conditions under PACE are satisfied. In any event the Constable may seize the weapon in question.

Section 1(4) provides a definition of an offensive weapon:

'Offensive weapon' means any article made or adapted for use for causing injury to the person, or intended by the person having it for such use by him (or some other person).

Hence, weapons become offensive in two ways:

(a) Some weapons are offensive because they have been made for the purpose of causing injury or have been so adapted.

(b) Any article which has the potential of causing injury is offensive if the possessor has it with the intention of causing injury.

The question of whether the article is offensive or not has an important bearing on the burden of proof: if the weapon is offensive and it can be proved that they had it with them in a public place, the burden shifts to the offender to prove that they had lawful authority or reasonable excuse.

Hence, for example, in the case of spray cans or improvised whips - unless it can be shown that they are offensive, by showing that they had the item with them with the intention of causing injury, they will not be classed as offensive weapons.

If a prosecution proves that the article is offensive, then they would have to prove, on the balance of possibilities, that they had a "reasonable excuse" for the possession, and this question of reasonableness is one for a jury.

Possession of a Controlled Drug

It is unlawful to have a controlled drug in your possession unless you have authorisation in the form of a licence, or if you did not know the substance was a controlled drug.

Three elements constitute the offence of possession:

The substance is in the possession or under the control of the individual. The substance must be in an individual's physical custody or under their control. This can include the substance being at the property of someone who is not present but has control over that property.

The individual knows the 'thing exists'. The individual must know of the existence of the substance and they must know that the substance is a controlled drug.

The substance is a controlled drug. The substance must in fact be a controlled drug. Therefore, if the individual thought they were in possession of cannabis but they were in fact in possession of tea leaves, no offence has been committed. Although there could be still a conviction for attempted possession.

It is a defence against a possession charge if the defendant can prove that, as soon as was practicable, they intended to destroy the substance or give it to someone who had legal authority to possess it.

The severity of the penalty applied in relation to drugs offences will depend on the individual circumstances of the case and the class of the drug. Below is a list of the more common drugs and their classification, Class A being the most severe.

Class A – heroin, methadone, crack, cocaine, ecstasy, magic mushrooms and 'crystal meth'

Class B – amphetamines, barbiturates and dihydrocodeine, Cannabis. Certain class B drugs are reclassified to Class A if they have been prepared for injection. These include amphetamines, dihydrocodeine and codeine.

Class C - benzodiazepines, steroids and subutex (buprenorphine).

Possession with intent to supply

It is an offence for a person to have a controlled drug in their possession, whether lawfully or not, with the intent to supply it to another. This offence is known as possession with intent to supply.

A person charged with possession with intent to supply can enter a plea of guilty to the charge of possession and not guilty to supply, on the grounds that the drugs seized were for personal use. At this point the prosecution may adduce evidence to attempt to prove guilt. Prosecutions for this offence may be based on circumstantial evidence, statements made by the defendant at the time of arrest and expert evidence.

Examples of relevant circumstantial evidence would include the possession of drug supply paraphernalia such as scales, bags, Clingfilm and large sums of unexplained cash. The manner in which the drugs were wrapped could also be used as evidence of intent to supply or to support the defendant's case (if the offence is denied) that the drugs were for personal use.

Statements at the time of arrest can be important. For example, a young person who is caught in possession of two ecstasy tablets and tells the Police, 'I was holding them for a friend,' could face a charge of possession with intent to supply.

In many cases the prosecution case will be built largely on the quantity of drugs seized, on the basis that the quantity was so large that it could not have been for personal use. Expert evidence can be crucial in such cases, to help the court to determine whether this is the case.

Criminal Damage

Criminal damage is where somebody damages an item or property. "A person who without lawful excuse destroys or damages any property belonging to another intending to destroy or damage any such property or being reckless as to whether any such property would be destroyed or damaged shall be guilty of an offence."

An example would be to break the windows on a bus shelter or to run a key down the side of a car, scratching the paintwork.

Theft

The act of stealing; specifically: the felonious taking and removing of personal property with intent to deprive the rightful owner of it.

A common example would be the theft of a bottle of wine from an off licence.

Robbery

The felonious taking of the property of another from his or her person or in his or her immediate presence, against his or her will, by violence or intimidation.

An example would be a teenager walking home is stopped by a group of teenagers and threatened with violence to hand over his mobile phone and mp3 player.

Common Assault

It is committed by a person who causes another person to apprehend the immediate use of unlawful violence by the defendant. This is any act by which a person intentionally or recklessly causes another to apprehend immediate unlawful violence. Such an act must be with the intent being calculated in that persons mind to cause apprehension or fear in the mind of the victim. Therefore, where there is no intent, there will be not be an assault, UNLESS, that the person who assaulted another, (and it was conclusive by way of evidence), that the person was indeed reckless as to the other person would in all probability have indeed apprehended that immediate unlawful violence would be used.

An assault is used to describe both an assault and battery, and indeed, there is often confusion between both the two offences.

Battery – contrary to section 39 of the Criminal Justice Act 1988

Common Assault – contrary to section 39 of the Criminal Justice Act 1988

Common assault and battery are summary offences, which means that the matter may only be tried in a Magistrates Court, and if found guilty have a maximum penalty not exceeding six months imprisonment or a fine not exceeding £5,000.00

However, an offence of common assault (to include battery) may be tried on indictment, that is the Crown Court.

An example may be:

A person throwing a wine bottle at another, and misses, will be an assault.

A person kicks another person causing no injury.

A person who uses a dog as a threat only, being an intention that the dog bite, but does not do so, will be an assault.

When assault is included to the term battery, this is defined as an act whereby a person intentionally or recklessly causes the other person to apprehend immediate unlawful personal violence or to sustain unlawful personal violence.

Battery is the act of intentionally or recklessly asserting unlawful force to another person.

Recklessness is common assault, which involves the foresight of the possibility that a person would fear immediate and unlawful violence, and that person takes the risk of doing the act. It is basically taking the risk, which is being reckless.

ABH

ABH is an assault that has caused a non-serious injury that has not broken the skin. In England and Wales, and in Northern Ireland, the offence is created by section 47 of the Offences against the Person Act 1861. "Whosoever shall be convicted upon an indictment of any assault occasioning ABH shall be liable ... to be kept in penal servitude".

An example would be somebody who has been punched in the face and has a black eye.

GBH

Grievous Bodily Harm is a more serious assault where a wound has been caused that breaks the skin. It comes under Section 18 and Section 20 of the Offences against the Person Act 1861.
Section 18 - "Whosoever shall unlawfully and maliciously by any means whatsoever wound or cause any grievous bodily harm to any person, with intent to do some grievous bodily harm to any person, or with intent to resist or prevent the lawful apprehension or detainee of any person, shall be guilty of an offence and, being convicted thereof, shall be liable to imprisonment for life."

Section 20 - "Whosoever shall unlawfully and maliciously wound or inflict any grievous bodily harm upon any other person, either with or without any weapon or instrument, shall be guilty of an offence and, being convicted therefore, shall be liable to a term of imprisonment not exceeding five years."

The two parts are for specific intent: Section 18 is wounding with intent and carries a harsher sentence.

An example would be where a knife has been used to stab somebody and caused a non-life-threatening injury and would be section 18. A section 20 could be causing a nosebleed to the injured party (IP) during a fight.

Burglary
Burglary is defined by section 9 of the Theft act 1968 which created two variants:
"A person is guilty of burglary if he enters any building or part of a building as a trespasser with intent to steal, inflict grievous bodily harm (or raping any person therein), or do unlawful damage to the building or anything in it. (section 9(1)(a))"

"A person is guilty of burglary if, having entered a building or part of a building as a trespasser, he steals or attempts to steal anything in the building, or inflicts or attempts to inflict grievous bodily harm on any person in the building (section 9(1)(b))"

For the crime to be complete certain elements outlined below need to be met.

Enters - although physical evidence of entry is not normally difficult to obtain, it can be difficult on occasions to decide whether an entry has occurred in law.

Building or part of a building - the Theft act 1968 does not define a building, so this must be a matter of fact for the jury, however, section 9(3) specifically states that the term includes an "inhabited vehicle or vessel"; hence motor homes, caravans and houseboats are protected by the section even when temporarily unoccupied. Burglary can also be committed in "part of a building" and in R v Walkington 1979 the defendant had entered a large shop during trading hours but went behind a counter and stole money from the till. The court held that he had entered that part of the building normally reserved for staff as a trespasser and was therefore guilty of burglary.

As a trespasser - the essence of trespass is entering or remaining on another's property without authority; a person having permission to enter property for one purpose who in fact enters for another purpose may become a trespasser: an example being, a friend invited you into their property and you then stole some jewelry. In recent years, the terms "distraction burglary", "artifice burglary" and "burglary by trick" have been used in crime prevention circles when access to premises is granted as a result of some deception on the occupier, usually by pretence that the burglar represents somebody who might reasonably request access such as a water, gas or electricity supplier. There is no separate legal definition of this variant.

With intent - the intention to commit an offence, being an essential element of burglary, requires proof beyond reasonable doubt. For example, if entry is made to regain property which the defendant honestly believes he has a right to take, there is no intention to steal and the defendant is entitled to be acquitted. However, it has been held that a conditional intent to steal anything found to be of value is enough to satisfy this requirement.

Sexual Assault

Sexual assault is an act of physical, psychological and emotional violation, in the form of a sexual act, which is inflicted on someone without consent. It can involve forcing or manipulating someone to witness or participate in any sexual acts, apart from penetration of the mouth with the penis, the penetration of anus or vagina (however slight) with any object or the penis, which is rape.

Rape

Rape is a type of sexual assault usually involving sexual intercourse, which is initiated by one or more persons against another person without that person's consent. A person who commits an act of rape is known as a rapist. The act may be carried out by physical force, coercion, abuse of authority or with a person who is incapable of valid consent
Rape is a crime that can have deep and profound effects on the victim and care needs to be taken both gaining witnesses details and taking sensitive samples.

The Sexual Offences Act 2003 (the Act) came into force on the 1st May 2004. The purpose of the Act was to strengthen and modernise the law on sexual offences, whilst improving preventative measures and the protection of individuals from sexual offenders. The Act extends the definition of rape to include the penetration by a penis of the vagina, anus or mouth of another person. The 2003 Act also changes the law about consent and belief in consent.

The word "consent" in the context of the offence of rape is now defined in the Sexual Offences Act 2003. A person consents if he or she agrees by choice, and has the freedom and capacity to make that choice. The essence of this definition is the agreement by choice. The law does not require the victim to have resisted physically in order to prove a lack of consent. The question of whether the victim consented is a matter for the jury to decide, although the Crown Prosecution Service (CPS) considers this issue very carefully throughout the life of the case.

Murder

Murder is the unlawful killing, with malice aforethought, of another human, and generally this state of mind distinguishes murder from other forms of killing such as manslaughter when there was no intent to kill. It is up to the CPS and jury to decide if there was the intent to kill.

Murder is an offence under the common law of England and Wales. It is considered the most serious form of homicide, in which one person kills another with the intention to unlawfully cause either death or serious injury. The element of intentionality was originally termed malice aforethought although it required neither malice nor premeditation. In certain circumstances intent can be 'transferred' when harm was intended to one person but a different person was killed, or acquired due to a common intent to commit serious harm with other people who go further and commit murder.

Manslaughter

Manslaughter is the unlawful killing of another person without the intention to kill or cause grievous bodily harm. Manslaughter is sally called either voluntary or involuntary. It is a common law crime under the offences against the person act 1861.

Voluntary where death follows an intended injury (but if the injury is serious, then this may be murder). It normally occurs as a result of sudden 'frying of temper' or following some degree of provocation.

Involuntary where injury is not intended, but nevertheless caused through gross negligence or an anlawful act.

A-Z OF COMMON OFFENCES IN ENGLAND AND WALES

• Abstracting Electricity (Sec. 13 Theft act 1968)

• Actual Bodily Harm (Sec. 47 Offences Against the Person Act)

• Affray (Sec. 3 Public Order Act 1984)

• Aggravated Burglary (Sec. 10 (1) Theft act 1986)

• Arson (Sec. 1 (3) Criminal Damage act 1971)

• Assault (Sec. 39 Criminal Justice act 1998)

• Assault On Police (Sec. 89 (1) Police Act 1996)

• Assault With Intent To Resist Arrest (Sec. 38 Offences Against The Person Act 1861)

• Assault With Intent To Rob (Sec. 8 (2) Theft act 1968)

• Bail (Sec. 6 Bail act 1976)

• Bail To A Police Station – Fail To Appear (Sec. 46 (a) Police and Criminal Evidence Act 1984)

• Battery (Sec. 39 Criminal Justice act 1998)

• Begging (Sec. 3 Vagrancy act 1824)

• Breach Of The Peace (common law)

- Burglary (Sec 9 (1a) Theft act 1968)

- Burglary (Sec 9 (1b) Theft act 1968)

- Chanting (Sec. 3 Football act 1991)

- Criminal Attempts (Sec. 1 Criminal Attempts act 1988)

- Criminal Damage (Sec. 1 (1) Criminal Damage act 1971)

- Criminal Damage - Possession Of Articles With Intent To Commit (Sec. 3 Criminal Damage Act 1971)

- Criminal Damage With Intent To Endanger Life (Sec. 1 (2) Criminal Damage act 1971)

- Criminal Damage - Threatening To Commit (Sec. 2 Criminal Damage act 1971)

- Disorderly Conduct (Sec. 18 Public Order Act 1986)

- Drunk And Disorderly (Sec. 91 (1) Criminal Justice act 1967)

- Drunk And Incapable (Sec. 12 Licensing act 1872)

- Encouraging Another to Murder (Sec. 4 Offences Against The Person Act 1861)

- Fear Of Provocation Of Violence (Sec. 4 Public Order Act 1984)

- Going Equipped (Sec. 25 (1) Theft act 1968)

- Grievous Bodily Harm or Unlawful Wounding (Sec. 20 Offences Against The Person Act 1861)

- Grievous Bodily Harm With Intent (Sec. 18 Offences Against The Person Act 1861)

- Handling Stolen Goods (Sec. 22 Theft act 1968)

- Harassment, Alarm or Distress (Sec. 5 Public Order Act 1984)

- Impersonation of a Police officer (Sec. 90 Police Act 1996)

- Indecent Assault (Sec. 14 (1) & 15 (1) Sexual Offences act 1956)

- Indecent Exposure (Sec. 4 Vagrancy act 1824)

- Injury or Assault to a Child (Sec. 1 Children and Young Persons act 1933) (amended 1989)

- Intentional Harassment, Alarm or Distress (Sec. 4(a) Public Order Act 1984)

- Kerb Crawling (Sec. 1 Sexual Offences act 1985)

- Making Off Without Payment (Sec. 3 (4) Theft act 1978)

- Manslaughter (common law)

- Mobile Telephones (road Vehicles (Construction and Use) (Amendment) (No. 4) Regulations 2003)

- Murder (common law)

- Obstruct Police (Sec. 89 (2) Police Act 1996)

- Obtaining Property By Deception (Sec. 15 (1) Theft act 1968)

- Obtaining services By Deception (Sec. 1 (1) Theft act 1968)

- Offensive Weapons – Possession Of (Sec. 1 Prevention Of Crime act 1953)

- Possession Of A Controlled Drug (Sec. 5 (2) Misuse Of Drugs act 1971)

- Possession Of A Controlled Drug With Intent To Supply (Sec. 5 (3) Misuse Of Drugs act 1971)

- Racially Aggravated Assault (Sec. 29 (1c) Crime And Disorder act 1998)

- Racially Aggravated Actual Bodily Harm (Sec. 29 (1b) Crime And Disorder act 1998)

- Racially Aggravated Criminal Damage (Sec. 30 (1) Crime And Disorder act 1998)

- Racially Aggravated Grievously Bodily Harm (Sec. 29 (1a) Crime And Disorder act 1998)

- Racially Aggravated Harassment (Sec. 32 1(a) Crime And Disorder act 1998)

- Rape (Sec. 1 Sexual Offences act 1956)

- Riot (Sec. 1 Public Order Act 1986)

- Robbery (Sec. 8 Theft act 1968)

- Theft (Sec. 1 (1) Theft act 1968)

- Violent Disorder (Sec. 2 Public Order Act 1986)

Road Traffic Offences

Road traffic offences are quite varied in their type and are covered by the Road Traffic Act 1988. In the main most offences are non-enforceable, but they come under two types:

Non-Endorsable - non-endorsable, or summary offences, are for less serious offences that carry a £30 or more fixed penalty, such as parking on double yellow lines, or not wearing a seatbelt. No points are received on the offender's driving license.

Summary Offence Codes

H159 Driver not in proper control of vehicle

H184 Failing to wear seatbelt (driver)

H185 Failing to wear seatbelt (passenger)

H246 VRM not conforming to regulation

H148 Misuse of fog lamps

H211 Fail to comply with Police no-waiting cone/sign

H074 Stopping on hard shoulder

H208 Stopping on clearway

H164 Driving elsewhere than on road

H192 Contravene mandatory keep left/right arrows

H015 Contravene bus lane

H276 Contravene route for tramcars only

H018 Contravene other statuary prohibition

H199 Waiting where un/loading prohibited

H200 Waiting where waiting prohibited

H204 Waiting in street-parking place longer than permitted

H209 Unnecessary obstruction

H210 Willful obstruction

H240 Parking in un/loading bay

H025 Parking in taxi rank

H026 Vehicle parked in residents parking bay

H028 Parking offside at night

H242 Cycling on footpath

Endorsable - these are more serious offences that carry a minimum of £60 fixed penalty and for which points are added to a licence. Examples are, using a mobile phone whilst driving (three points), and driving without insurance (six to eight points and up to £5000 fine).

Endorsable Offences and Codes
Accident Offences

AC10 Failing to stop after an accident

AC20 Failing to give particulars or to report an accident within 24 hours

AC30 Undefined accident offences

Disqualified Driver

BA10   Driving whilst disqualified by order of court

BA30   Attempting to drive whilst disqualified by order of court

Careless Driving

CD10   Driving without due care and attention

CD20 Driving without reasonable consideration for other road users

CD30 Driving without due care and attention or without reasonable consideration for other road users

CD40 Causing death through careless driving when unfit through drink

CD50 Causing death by careless driving when unfit through drugs

CD60 Causing death by careless driving with alcohol level above the limit

CD70 Causing death by careless driving then failing to supply a specimen for analysis

Construction & Use Offences

CU10 Using a vehicle with defective brakes

CU20 Causing or likely to cause danger by reason of use of unsuitable vehicle or using a vehicle with parts or accessories (excluding brakes, steering or tires) in a dangerous condition

CU30 Using a vehicle with defective tyre(s)

CU40 Using a vehicle with defective steering

CU50 Causing or likely to cause danger by reason of load or passengers

CU80 Using a mobile phone whilst driving a motor vehicle

Reckless/Dangerous Driving

DD40 Dangerous Driving

DD60 Manslaughter or culpable homicide whilst driving a vehicle

DD80 Causing death by dangerous driving

Drink or Drugs

DR10 Driving or attempting to drive with alcohol level above limit

DR20 Driving or attempting to drive whilst unfit through drink

DR30 Driving or attempting to drive then failing to supply a specimen for analysis

DR40 In charge of a vehicle whilst alcohol level above limit

DR50 In charge of a vehicle whilst unfit through drink

DR60 Failure to provide a specimen for analysis in circumstances other than driving or attempting to drive

DR70 Failing to provide specimen for breathe test

DR80 Driving or attempting to drive when unfit through drugs

DR90 In charge of a vehicle when unfit through drugs

Insurance Offences

IN10 Using a vehicle uninsured against third party risks

Licence Offences

LC20 Driving otherwise than in accordance with a licence

LC30 Driving after making a false declaration about fitness when applying for a licence

LC40 Driving a vehicle having failed to notify a disability

LC50 Driving after a licence has been revoked or refused on medical grounds

Miscellaneous Offences

MS10 Leaving a vehicle in a dangerous position

MS20 Unlawful pillion riding

MS30 Play street offences

MS40 Driving with uncorrected defective eyesight or refusing to submit to a test

MS50 Motor racing on the highway

MS60 Offences not covered by other codes

MS70 Driving with uncorrected defective eyesight

MS80 Refusing to submit to an eyesight test

MS90 Failure to give information as to identity of driver, etc

Motorway Offences

MW10 Contravention of Special Roads Regulations (excluding speed limits)

Pedestrian Crossings

PC10 Undefined Contravention of Pedestrian Crossing Regulations

PC20 Contravention of Pedestrian Crossing Regulations with moving vehicle

PC30 Contravention of Pedestrian Crossing Regulations with stationary vehicle

Speed Limits

SP10 Exceeding goods vehicle speed limits

SP20 Exceeding speed limit for type of vehicle (excluding goods or passenger vehicles)

SP30 Exceeding statutory speed limit on a public road

SP40 Exceeding passenger vehicle speed limit

SP50 Exceeding speed limit on a motorway

SP60 Undefined speed limit offence

Traffic Direction and Signs

TS10 Failing to comply with traffic light signals

TS20 Failing to comply with double white lines

TS30 Failing to comply with "Stop" sign

TS40 Failing to comply with direction of a Constable/warden

TS50 Failing to comply with traffic sign (excluding - stop - signs, traffic lights or double white lines)

TS60 Failing to comply with a school crossing patrol sign

TS70 Undefined failure to comply with a traffic direction sign

Special Code

TT99 To signify a disqualification under totting up procedure. If the total of penalty points reaches 12 or more within three years, the driver is liable to be disqualified.

Theft or Unauthorised Taking

UT50 Aggravated taking of a vehicle

Some common driving offences are listed below:

Drink Driving

The offence - it is an offence for you to drive - or even attempt to drive - a motor vehicle when you are unfit to do so as a result of consuming drink or drugs. Section 5 of the Road Traffic Act 1988 specifically provides that you will be guilty of an offence if you either:

Drive or attempt to drive a motor vehicle on a road or other public place, or

are in charge of a motor vehicle on a road or other public place.

This is after consuming so much alcohol that the proportion of it in your breath, blood or urine exceeds the prescribed limit.

Maximum Penalty - a maximum penalty of six months imprisonment, a fine of up to £5,000 and a minimum 12 month driving ban.

The penalty for refusing to provide a specimen of breath, blood or urine for analysis is a maximum six months imprisonment, up to £5000 fine and a driving ban of at least 12 months.

Comment - the offence of driving whilst under the influence of alcohol is one to which there is no defence, as such. However, it may be possible to argue that special reasons exist which are such that you should not be disqualified from driving, despite having committed the offence.

The current limits are:

35 micrograms of alcohol in 100 ml of breath

80 milligrams of alcohol in 100 ml of blood

107 milligrams of alcohol in 100 ml of urine

Failing to Stop/Give Particulars after an accident (AC10) (AC20)

The offence - being the driver of a mechanically propelled vehicle, owing to the presence of which on a road an accident occurred whereby personal injury or damage was caused to another person or another vehicle or an animal not in the vehicle, or property on or near the road, then failed to stop or on being required by a person to give your name and address and the name and address of the owner and the identity mark of the vehicle, failed to do so.

Maximum Penalty - six months imprisonment and/or a fine not exceeding £5000. Endorsement with 5 to 10 penalty points. Discretionary disqualification.

Comment - they only have to stop and give particulars if someone or something (not in the other vehicle) is injured in the incident, or if they cause any damage to another vehicle or to anything else on or by the roadside (e.g. a lamp post, fence or wall).

The likelihood of being imprisoned increases with the severity of the accident, and if there is both a failure to stop and a failure to report the accident, if:

a) the Court believes that this was because you were trying to avoid a breath test, or

b) when serious injury is caused.

If you can satisfy the court that you were unaware that an accident had occurred this may be a defence to the charge.

Failing to Report an Accident
The offence - being the driver of a mechanically propelled vehicle, owing to the presence of which on a road an accident occurred whereby personal injury was caused to another person, and not having given your name and address to a person having reasonable grounds for requiring you to do so, failed to report the accident at a Police station or to a Constable as soon as reasonably practicable and in any case within 24 hours of the occurrence of the accident.
Maximum Penalty - six months imprisonment and/or fine not exceeding £5000. Endorsement with 5 to 10 penalty points. Discretionary disqualification.

Speeding/Exceeding the speed limit (SP30)
Offence - driving on a road exceeding the prescribed speed limit.
Maximum penalty - fine not exceeding £1000. Endorsement with 3 to 6 penalty points. Discretionary disqualification.

Comment - if they are doing more than 30 mph over the limit they are very likely to be disqualified, depending on speed, road traffic conditions, weather, etc.

If you are offered a fixed penalty option, and you are guilty then you are probably best to take this option, as your licence will be endorsed with the minimum number of penalty points and the fine is likely to be less than that imposed by the court. There will also be no court fees.

Possible defences are that they were not speeding, that it was not them driving, or that they were driving an exempted vehicle in an emergency.

The prosecution may obtain a conviction by producing in evidence photographs taken from speed cameras. There is no requirement that such photos have any other evidence to back them up. If no photo is available then the evidence to convict must come from at least two different sources, although one of these may be mechanical, such as the Police car's speedometer/radar gun/VASCAR. Under s20 of the road Traffic Offenders act (as amended by s23 of the Road Traffic Act 1991), where a radar device is used the Police merely need to provide a record produced by the prescribed device AND (in the same or a separate document) a certificate as to the circumstances in which the record was produced, signed by Constable or authorised person.

Driving Without Insurance
The Offence - you will commit an offence if you use, or to let another person use, a motor vehicle on a road or public place which does not have in force in respect of it an insurance policy

which at the very least insures against third party risks and which complies with section 143 of the Road Traffic Act 1988.

Maximum Penalty - fine not exceeding £5000. Endorsement with 6 to 8 penalty points. Discretionary disqualification.

Totting up - under the totting up provisions a driver can be disqualified when he/she accumulates a certain number of penalty points within a three year period. The 'magic' number is 12.

If you reach 12 penalty points within the three year period (and it is the date of the offences and NOT the date of the hearings that is relevant), then you will be disqualified for a minimum period of six months.

If you are then disqualified the slate is wiped clean of points on the date you get your licence back.

To avoid being banned for totting up, you will need to be able to convince the court that there are 'mitigating circumstances'. This means that you will have to show that a disqualification would cause exceptional hardship. The loss of your job could be considered to be exceptional hardship. This could extend to the loss of employment for others dependant on you, or hardship to members of your family.

A new driver only needs to gain six points within two years of passing their test to receive a ban and needing to retake their test.

Dangerous Driving
The main types of driving offences involving fatalities are more often than not 'dangerous driving' and 'careless or inconsiderate

driving'. The driver's behaviour is what is important, not what the driver believes. Someone may be committing a dangerous driving offence even though they believe they are driving safely. The offence is often based around other people's perceptions and any other evidence. For example the scene of the crash can yield evidence if the dangerous driving led to a RTC.

A person drives dangerously when:
The way they drive falls far below the minimum acceptable standard expected of a competent and careful driver; and it would be obvious to a competent and careful driver that driving in that way would be dangerous.

Some typical examples from court cases of dangerous driving are:

Racing, going too fast, or driving aggressively

Ignoring traffic lights, road signs or warnings from passengers

Overtaking dangerously

Driving under the influence of drink or drugs, including prescription drugs

Driving when unfit, including having an injury, being unable to see clearly, not taking prescribed drugs, or being sleepy

Knowing the vehicle has a dangerous fault or an unsafe load

The driver being avoidably and dangerously distracted, for example by:

Using a hand-held phone or other equipment

Reading, or looking at a map

Talking to and looking at a passenger

Lighting a cigarette, changing a CD or tape, tuning the radio.

Dangerous or Inconsiderate Driving
A person drives carelessly or inconsiderately when the way they drive falls below the minimum acceptable standard expected of a competent and careful driver.

Some examples of careless driving are:

Overtaking on the inside

Driving too close to another vehicle

Driving through a red light by mistake

Turning into the path of another vehicle

The driver being avoidably distracted by tuning the radio, lighting a cigarette etc.

Examples of inconsiderate driving include:

Flashing lights to force other drivers to give way

Misusing lanes to gain advantage over other drivers

Unnecessarily staying in an overtaking lane

Unnecessarily slow driving or braking

Dazzling other drivers with un-dipped headlights

Number Plate Offences
Number plate offences are quite common and sometimes they
are done intentionally and sometimes by naivety. With the use of
ANPR systems the importance of having the correct type of
number plate has been seen as even more important.

The basic rules for number plates:

You must display a number plate on the front and rear of your
vehicle

Letters should be black on a white plate at the front

Letters should be black on a yellow plate at the rear

The background surface should be reflex-reflecting, but not the
letters

Number plates should meet the British Standard

Rules on character dimensions differ slightly depending on
whether your plates were fitted before or after 1st September
2001. Details are below.

Rules on character dimensions differ for traditional 'black and
white' plates, which may be fitted on vehicles manufactured
before 1st January 1973.

Any number plate made up after 1st September 2001 must meet the dimensions below:

Character Height 79 mm

Character Width (except the figure 1 or letter I) 50 mm

Character stroke 14 mm

Space between characters 11 mm

Space between groups 33 mm

Top, bottom, and side margins (minimum) 11 mm

Space between vertical lines 19 mm

Most offences are usually around not having the correct font or incorrect spacing. Other offences include using screws to alter a letter or number or the use of black or pressed plates.

Number plates that are incorrect can either be dealt with a Vehicle Defect Rectification Summons (VDRS) that will mean the vehicle owner will need to change the number plates and then get an MOT centre stamp a certificate. Which is then taken to their nearest police station, to verify that the plates are now correct. The other alternative is to issue a fixed penalty notice and request that the plates be changed to the correct format via a VDRS as well.

On private registrations the DVLA have a form for the number plate infringement to be reported. If caught on a second occasion they can then have the registration taken off of them.

DOMESTIC VIOLENCE

Domestic violence is sadly a common occurrence and one that can have lasting physiological effects on families. Being able to read the warning signs and take positive action is essential for any Police officer. Constabulary's now have robust domestic violence Polices in the light of tragic cases such as Casey Brittle, where Police missed opportunities to save the life of a young mother who was murdered by her violent ex-partner.

Casey was kicked and punched to death in front of her two-year-old daughter after suffering years of abuse. The little girl walked into the room where her father Sanchez Williams was carrying out the attack and afterwards stayed with her unconscious mother for two hours. Miss Brittle was so scared of her ex-partner she 'played down' the incidents and was reluctant to press charges. As a result, Williams was never charged with a criminal offence in relation to her and the violence eventually escalated to murder. It is essential that a risk assessment is done with any domestic and that the relevant third parties are informed. Many forces have their own domestic violence units or will offer support and help to the victim. It is important to use you own perception as well. Does it feel right? Is there anything that seems not add up? If in doubt seek advice from a supervisor or even the domestic violence unit itself.

A domestic incident can be between family members as well as current and ex-partners. The first action at any domestic is safeguarding the victim and any children involved. This may mean arresting the abuser or removing them from the property/locality. It could mean taking the victim and/or children to a place of safety. Second is to carry out a thorough investigation and involve partner agencies where necessary. To ensure no escalation of domestic violence occurs and robust measures are put in place to ensure safety and wellbeing of the victim.

Incidence and prevalence of domestic violence:
Domestic violence accounts for between 16% and one quarter of all recorded violent crime.
One incident is reported to the Police every minute.

45% women and 26% men had experienced at least one incident of inter-personal violence in their lifetimes. However when there were more than 4 incidents (i.e. ongoing domestic or sexual abuse) 89% of victims were women.

In any one year, there are 13 million separate incidents of physical violence or threats of violence against women from partners or former partners.

Women are much more likely than men to be the victim of multiple incidents of abuse, and of sexual violence: 32% of women who had ever experienced domestic violence did so four or five (or more) times, compared with 11% of the (smaller number) of men who had ever experienced domestic violence; and women constituted 89% of all those who had experienced 4 or more incidents of domestic violence.

Women are more likely than men to have experienced all types of intimate violence (partner abuse, family abuse, sexual assault and stalking) since the ages of 16. And nearly half the woman who had experienced intimate violence of any kind, were likely to have been victims of more than one kind of intimate abuse.

54% of UK rapes are committed by a woman's current or former partner.

On average 2 women a week are killed by a male partner or former partner: this constitutes around one-third of all female homicide victims.

All forms of domestic abuse have one purpose which is to gain and maintain control over the victim. Abusers use many tactics to exert power over their spouse or partner: dominance, humiliation, isolation, threats, intimidation, denial and blame.

Distinctions need to be made regarding types of violence, motives of perpetrators, and the social and cultural context. Violence by a person against their intimate partner is often done as a way for controlling "their partner", even if this kind of violence is not the most frequent. Other types of intimate partner violence also occur, including violence between gay and lesbian couples, and by women against their male partners.

Distinctions are not based on single incidents, but rather on patterns across numerous incidents and motives of the perpetrator.

Different Types of Abuse

Physical abuse
Physical abuse is abuse involving contact intended to cause feelings of intimidation, pain, injury, or other physical suffering or bodily harm.
Physical abuse includes hitting, slapping, punching, choking, pushing, and other types of contact that result in physical injury to the victim. Physical abuse can also include behaviors such as

denying the victim of medical care when needed, depriving the victim of sleep or other functions necessary to live, or forcing the victim to engage in drug/alcohol use against his/her will.] It can also include inflicting physical injury onto other targets, such as children or pets, in order to cause psychological harm to the victim.

Sexual Abuse

Sexual abuse is any situation in which force or threat is used to obtain participation in unwanted sexual activity. Coercing a person to engage in sex, against their will, even if that person is a spouse or intimate partner with whom consensual sex has occurred, is an act of aggression and violence.

Sexual violence is defined by World Health Organization as: any sexual act, attempt to obtain a sexual act, unwanted sexual comments or advances, or acts to traffic, or otherwise directed, against a person's sexuality using coercion, by any person regardless of their relationship to the victim, in any setting, including but not limited to home and work.

Marital rape, also known as spousal rape, is non-consensual sex in which the perpetrator is the victim's spouse. As such, it is a form of partner rape, of domestic violence, and of sexual abuse.

Categories of sexual abuse include:

Use of physical force to compel a person to engage in a sexual act against his or her will, whether or not the act is completed;

Attempted or completed sex act involving a person who is unable to understand the nature or condition of the act, unable to decline participation, or unable to communicate unwillingness to engage in the sexual act, e.g., because of underage immaturity, illness, disability, or the influence of alcohol or other drugs, or because of intimidation or pressure.

Emotional

Emotional abuse (also called psychological abuse or mental abuse) can include humiliating the victim privately or publicly, controlling what the victim can and cannot do, withholding information from the victim, deliberately doing something to make the victim feel diminished or embarrassed, isolating the victim from friends and family, implicitly blackmailing the victim by harming others when the victim expresses independence or happiness, or denying the victim access to money or other basic resources and necessities.

Emotional abuse can include verbal abuse and is defined as any behavior that threatens, intimidates, undermines the victim's self-worth or self-esteem, or controls the victim's freedom. This can include threatening the victim with injury or harm, telling the victim that they will be killed if they ever leave the relationship, and public humiliation. Constant criticism, name-calling, and making statements that damage the victim's self-esteem are also common verbal forms of emotional abuse. Often perpetrators will use children to engage in emotional abuse by teaching them to harshly criticize the victim as well. Emotional abuse includes conflicting actions or statements which are designed to confuse and create insecurity in the victim. These behaviors also lead the victim to question themselves, causing them to believe that they are making up the abuse or that the abuse is their fault.

Emotional abuse includes forceful efforts to isolate the victim, keeping them from contacting friends or family. This is intended to eliminate those who might try to help the victim leave the relationship and to create a lack of resources for them to rely on if they were to leave. Isolation results in damaging the victim's sense of internal strength, leaving them feeling helpless and unable to escape from the situation.

People who are being emotionally abused often feel as if they do not own themselves; rather, they may feel that their significant other has nearly total control over them. Women or men undergoing emotional abuse often suffer from depression, which puts them at increased risk for suicide, eating disorders, and drug and alcohol abuse.

Verbal

Verbal abuse is a form of emotionally abusive behavior involving the use of language. It may include profanity but can occur with or without the use of expletives.

Verbal abuse may include aggressive actions such as name-calling, blaming, ridicule, disrespect, and criticism, but there are also less obviously aggressive forms of verbal abuse. Statements that may seem benign on the surface can be thinly veiled attempts to humiliate; falsely accuse; or manipulate others to submit to undesirable behavior; make others feel unwanted and unloved; threaten others economically; or isolate victims from support systems.

In Jekyll and Hyde behaviors, the abuser may fluctuate between sudden rages and false joviality toward the victim; or may simply show a very different "face" to the outside world than to the victim. While oral communication is the most common form of verbal abuse, it includes abusive communication in written form.

Economic

Economic abuse is a form of abuse when one intimate partner has control over the other partner's access to economic resources. Economic abuse may involve preventing a spouse from resource acquisition, limiting the amount of resources to use by the victim, or by exploiting economic resources of the victim.

The motive behind preventing a spouse from acquiring resources is to diminish victim's capacity to support himself/herself, thus forcing him/her to depend on the perpetrator financially, which includes preventing the victim from obtaining education, finding employment, maintaining or advancing their careers, and acquiring assets. In addition, the abuser may also put the victim on an allowance, closely monitor how the victim spends money, spend victim's money without his/her consent and creating debt, or completely spend victim's savings to limit available resources

Children

On children there has been an increase in acknowledgment that a child who is exposed to domestic abuse during their upbringing will suffer in their developmental and psychological welfare. Due to the awareness of domestic violence that some children have to face, it also generally impacts how the child develops emotionally, socially, behaviorally as well as cognitively. Some emotional and behavioral problems that can result due to domestic violence include increased aggressiveness, anxiety, and changes in how a child socializes with friends, family, and authorities. Depression, as well as self-esteem issues, can follow due to traumatic experiences. Problems with attitude and cognition in schools can start developing, along with a lack of skills such as problem-solving. Correlation has been found between the experience of abuse and neglect in childhood and perpetrating domestic violence and sexual abuse in adulthood. Additionally, in some cases the abuser will purposely abuse the mother in front of the child to cause a ripple effect, hurting not one but two of his victims. It has been found that children who witness mother-assault are more likely to exhibit symptoms of posttraumatic stress disorder (PTSD).

Long Term Effects

Physical Bruises, broken bones, head injuries, lacerations, and internal bleeding are some of the acute effects of a domestic violence incident that require medical attention and hospitalization. Some chronic health conditions that have been linked to victims of domestic violence are arthritis, irritable bowel syndrome, chronic pain, pelvic pain, ulcers, and migraines. Victims who are pregnant during a domestic violence relationship experience greater risk of miscarriage, pre-term labor, and injury to or death of the fetus. Psychological among victims who are still living with their perpetrators, high amounts of stress, fear, and anxiety are commonly reported. Depression is also common, as victims are made to feel guilty for 'provoking' the abuse and are constantly subjected to intense criticism. It is reported that 60% of victims meet the diagnostic criteria for depression, either during or after termination of the relationship, and have a greatly increased risk of suicidality. In addition to depression, victims of domestic violence also commonly experience long-term anxiety and panic, and are likely to meet the diagnostic criteria for Generalized Anxiety Disorder and Panic Disorder. The most commonly referenced psychological effect of domestic violence is PTSD. PTSD (as experienced by victims) is characterized by flashbacks, intrusive images, exaggerated startle response, nightmares, and avoidance of triggers that are associated with the abuse. These symptoms are generally experienced for a long span of time after the victim has left the dangerous situation. Many researchers state that PTSD is possibly the best diagnosis for those suffering from psychological effects of domestic violence, as it accounts for the variety of symptoms commonly experienced by victims of trauma.

Financial concerns are once victims leave their perpetrator, they can be stunned with the reality of the extent to which the abuse has taken away their autonomy. Due to economic abuse and isolation, the victim usually has very little money of their own and few people on whom they can rely when seeking help. This has been shown to be one of the greatest obstacles facing victims of domestic violence, and the strongest factor that can discourage them from leaving their perpetrators. In addition to lacking financial resources, victims of domestic violence often lack specialized skills, education, and training that are necessary to find gainful employment, and also may have several children to support. It has also been reported that one out of every three homeless women are homeless due to having left a domestic violence relationship. If a victim is able to secure rental housing, it is likely that her apartment complex will have "zero tolerance" policies for crime; these policies can cause them to face eviction even if they are the victim (not the perpetrator) of violence. While the number of shelters and community resources available to domestic violence victims has grown tremendously, these agencies often have few employees and hundreds of victims seeking assistance which causes many victims to remain without the assistance they need.

WITNESS STATEMENTS

A large proportion of Police time is taken up in writing statements. These may be for the IP or from a Police officer who has seized an item from a crime scene, made an arrest or even a witness themselves. In this chapter we shall look at how to write a statement, go through what needs to be included and we'll look at some examples.

What is a Statement?

A statement is a pen picture of an incident or event. It needs to be detailed enough so that anyone reading it that was not at the scene can get a detailed picture of what went on: it also needs to meet the requirements of the CPS.

Witness statements are just one of the sources of factual information used by the Police and CPS to determine what actually happened in an incident, if there was a violation of the rules, and what penalty is appropriate.

The balance of a statement should record the version of the facts, what was heard and seen. Do not include any information from other people.

It is important that each witness writes his/her statement, as it is unlikely that each witness saw every part of the incident or saw it from the same physical perspective and there will therefore be significant differences in the statements. Unfortunately, this does make for more paperwork, but it ensures that more facts are available to make the right decision.

Avoid deductions, conclusions, or opinions, as they are not facts. If you use words such as "I think" or "it appeared" or "probably", you are conveying to the statement reader that you did not observe but are deducing, forming an opinion or concluding what you think you may have seen, and these statements could be given less consideration or discounted completely as not being factual. Present the details that you used to form an opinion, not the opinion itself. For example, you could say, "car A changed his line and suddenly moved left into the right side of car B" but not, "car A intentionally hit car B".

We will start with an acronym that needs to roll off the tongue and will make life so much easier when writing statements that include a description of a suspect.

"ADVOKATE"

A Amount of time the incident was seen for.

D Distance from incident.

V Visibility - was it dark or sunny? Were street lights on? Was it night or day?

O Obstructions - did a tree or lampost, etc obstruct your/their view?

K Known or unknown - have you seen these people before and do you know them?

A Any reason to remember, e.g., unique points that make this memorable.

T Time Lapse - how much time has elapsed since the witness saw the incident/suspect.

E Error or material discrepancy - any differences between the description given by the witness and the actual appearance of the suspect.

When doing any witness statement try to include all of the points if applicable. Below are two example statements: the first is just an account and is too brief, the second is the same statement showing how it should be done.

One of the main issues Police officers intially find in doing statements is the level of detail that needs to be included. Practice is the key to writing good statements.

I am Police Constable 1234 Rockitt of the Anytown Police, currently stationed at Any Station. I was on duty in full uniform with PC 8808 ANDERSON on 22nd May 2009 at 22:55.

When we were stationary at the traffic lights at the side of the Dog and Cat Pub Anytown we observed a group of white males pushing and attempting to punch each other. One Male I noticed punching and shoving was who I now know to be John Doe DOB 16/07/72 IC1 Male, shaved head, wearing a White Jumper and Blue Jeans approx 6 feet tall. Once the lights had changed to Green we went round to the front of the DOG AND CAT PUB and on leaving the Police Car I noticed DOE push another male who I could not see fully due to it being blocked by the building. Then on at 23:00 on that day (22/05/09) went over and attempted to arrest DOE for affray and said "I am arresting you for affray" CAUTIONED to which he said "I HAVE NOT DONE ANYTHING" then resisted arrest by trying to shake me loose and replied "I have not done anything fuck off" and continued to resist by pulling away even though I had my right hand on his left arm and left hand on his wrist. I noticed that he was heavily in drink and difficult to handle. At this point several of the males became hostile and tried to prevent me arresting DOE and his girlfriend Christine JONES DOB 03/02/72 IC1 Female with Blonde Hair White top and back skirt, black tights and black heeled boots tried to pull DOE away from me. On pulling away I was pulled to the ground and at this point fearing for my safety I pressed the panic button and requested backup. PC8808 ANDERSON tried to move the crowd away and regain control. At this point DOE and JONES moved to the front of the DOG AND CAT PUB and continued to resist me arresting DOE at this point PC 999 ARREST arrived to give assistance and I drew my ASP to move the crowd away and told the to "Back off" at this point I noticed JONES kick PC 999 ARREST on the right leg to the knee. With further backup DOE was removed from JONES I arrested him still being abusive swearing and trying to resist arrest. DOE was then conveyed to the Custody.

This statement is for a large fight outside a pub but is far too short and lacks ADVOKATE fully, lacks detail as it is not a detailed pen picture. Setting the scene and describing the area and offenders was too brief.

Below are how the statement should have be written and the level of detail required.

I am Police Constable 1234 ROCKITT based at ANY STATION Police Station ANYTOWN for ANYTOWN POLICE. At 22:55 hours on Friday 6th March 2009 I was conducting uniformed patrol duties in company with SC 8088 ANDERSON in the ANYTOWN area. At this time I was driving a fully liveried Police vehicle along LONG ROAD,

ANYTOWN and was waiting to turn right onto SHORT ROAD at the traffic lights.

The DOG AND CAT PUB public house known locally as the DOG AND CAT PUB was located on my right hand side. The property fronts onto LONG ROAD, one side is adjacent to SHORT ROAD and the rear of this public house backs onto END ROAD. To my right I noticed a large group of males, approximately 10 – 12 males, that were on the pavement between the side of the DOG AND CAT PUB and the safety railings. There looked to be two separate groups and I could see about four people jostling each other. The four were behaving aggressively towards each other and they looked like they were being abusive, their faces were contorted and confrontational to each other. I observed this group whilst waiting at the traffic lights for about two minutes and became concerned that a fight was breaking out, as the group continued to jostle each other and I feared things were going to escalate. I passed on what I had seen to Command and Control via my radio.

I would estimate the group were 20 feet away from me and I had a clear unobstructed view of the group. The weather was clear and the street lighting illuminated the streets to a good degree. I saw a male in a grey top throw a punch at a male in a white top. From now on I will refer to the male in the grey top as male 1. The male in the white top I now know to be John DOE DOB 16/09/1973. I would describe DOE as a white male with a shaved head and approximately 6 feet tall. DOE was of a medium build and spoke with a local accent aged in his early thirties. DOE was wearing a knitted white polo neck jumper and plain dark blue jeans.

Male 1 I would describe as white and of medium build, he was between 5'08" and 5'10" tall. Aged in his early thirties he had short cropped dark hair and he was wearing a short sleeved grey t-shirt with white piping around the neck area. I have not seen this male before nor do I know him, but I would recognise him again.

DOE then shoved male 1 away, causing him to stumble backwards. Male one then came forward again and tried to throw another punch at DOE. DOE then lunged forward towards male 1 and at this point the traffic lights changed and I moved off to park the Police vehicle on LONG ROAD. I lost visual contact with the group for about one minute whilst parking the vehicle in a safe place.

I then got out of the Police vehicle by the railings on LONG ROAD opposite the entrance to the public house. I saw the same group of people standing on the pavement by SHORT ROAD, however, I could only see three people at this stage. I could see DOE, he was about 30 feet away from where I was standing with no obstructions. I saw DOE use both his arms to push another male, hard. DOE appeared to push the male deliberately with significant force.

At 23:00 hours I ran over to DOE and said "I am arresting you for affray" CAUTION to which he said "I'VE NOT DONE ANYTHING, WE'RE JUST MESSING AROUND!" I put my right hand on DOE's left shoulder and my left hand on DOE's right wrist in a prisoner escort technique to lead DOE away from the scene to diffuse the situation. DOE immediately resisted my attempt to lead him away from the scene by standing still and tensing his body. DOE was heavily into drink, I could smell intoxicating liqueur on his breath and his eyes were watery.

183

DOE was very aggressive in both his manner and tone. DOE had an aggressive look in his eyes as if he had just been involved in a fight or heated argument with another person.

At this point I became surrounded by a number of males who began to shout at me "HE HASN'T DONE ANYTHING!" At least two males got within 15 centimeters of my face and repeatedly shouted ""HE HASN'T DONE ANYTHING!". I immediately began to be concerned for the safety of SC ANDERSON and myself at this point. The males had closed down my reactionary gap and were becoming increasingly hostile. I still had DOE in an escort hold.

At this point a white female approached, who I now know to be Christine JONES DOB 03/02/1972 who I would describe as having shoulder length or longer blonde hair, of slim build aged in her thirties, around 5'04" – 5'06" tall . JONES was wearing a white t-shirt type top, black skirt, and black tights with black heeled boots and came to the left side of me and threw her arms around DOE's waist in order to prevent me from taking DOE away. JONES who appeared quite emotional continued to violently pull at DOE's waist causing him to fall backwards, onto the pavement. JONES also fell onto her back and DOE fell onto JONES. I kept hold of DOE to try and prevent him from falling over with JONES. This pulled me off balance and dragged me down to the point where I was down on one knee. I immediately let go of DOE as I was now very concerned and felt both PC 8088 ANDERSON and myself were in grave danger. I immediately pressed my emergency button on the Airwave radio to summon assistance.

I managed to get back to my feet and I saw SC ANDERSON shout loudly at the crowd. "WILL YOU GET BACK ! The crowd then moved around towards the front door of the DOG AND CAT PUB, JONES was still holding onto DOE and they were resting up against the side of the DOG AND CAT PUB.

I would estimate there were now about 12 – 14 people out on the pavement in front of the DOG AND CAT PUB. PC 999 ARREST arrived and he was standing less than two feet in front of JONES and DOE. He attempted to split up JONES and DOE, JONES reacted and kicked PC 999 ARREST in a toe poke frontward kick to PC 999 ARREST's right knee to make him back off.

PC ARREST backed away so as to prevent further assault. As he did this the crowd began to shout angrily and aggressively "DON'T TOUCH HER SHE IS A WOMAN!" Both PC 999 ARREST and myself were totally surrounded by the crowd who were increasingly hostile towards Police. I became fearful for my safety so I withdrew my Police issue ASP baton and placed the baton over my right shoulder and shouted at the crowd "BACK OFF! BACK OFF! BACK OFF! BACK OFF!" I felt the situation was escalating and getting out of control.

Other officers arrived very quickly and began to disperse the crowd. I located DOE shortly after the initial crowd had been dispersed and reminded DOE he was under arrest for affray. I handcuffed DOE to the rear and double locked the handcuffs and checked for tightness. C division officers then conveyed DOE to the CUSTODY suite in a marked Police van.

At this time there was still a large crowd with parts of the crowd still hostile. I was advised that there was already a prisoner in our Police vehicle. Then in company with PC ANDERSON I conveyed a male I now know to be Antony WOOD into

CUSTODY where the custody sergeant authorised his detention.

Later I returned to the DOG AND CAT PUB with PC 8088 ANDERSON who seized CCTV footage from the premises.

I shall now outline some key points from the statement. You will notice all surnames are in capitals as are any quotes so that they stand out, the description of the offender is written first by physical description, then by clothes.

"John DOE DOB 16/09/1973. I would describe DOE as a white male with a shaved head and approximately 6 feet tall. DOE was of a medium build and spoke with a local accent aged in his early thirties. DOE was wearing a knitted white polo neck jumper and plain dark blue jeans."

Seizure Statement
Here is an example of a seizure statement. Whenever you seize anything that is part of a crime or investigation a statement must be written.

I am a Police Constable 1234 ROCKITT of ANYTOWN Police currently stationed at ANYSTATION.

I was on duty in full uniform on 7th September 2008 at 20:00 when I attended 124 ACACIA road, ANYTOWN to assist other officers in the execution of a search warrant as part of an ongoing investigation. Whilst at the address I seized the following items.

Seized four mobile phones and I refer to these as Police item JR/1 Nokia mobile phone, JR/2 Sony Ericson mobile phone,

JR/3 Samsung mobile phone, JR/3 Blackberry mobile phone from the front left bedroom under a pile of clothes in the left hand corner next to the bed.

I subsequently handed these exhibits to PC999 ARREST, the exhibits officer.

Basic Arrest Statement
I am a Police Constable 1234 ROCKITT of ANYTOWN Police currently stationed at ANYSTATION.
I was on duty in full uniform on 3rd August 2008 at 19:45 I was on duty with SC 8088 ANDERSON.

At 19:45 on that day (03/09/08) I attended the address of Jane DOE born 18/12/68 of 53 COLLEGE Street, ANYTOWN.

As a result of two witness statements gathered earlier the same day, I said to DOE "I am arresting you on suspicion of criminal damage at 55a COLLEGE Street, ANYTOWN.

CAUTIONED.

DOE made no reply to the caution.

DOE was then conveyed to custody where her detention was authorised.

At 21:38 hours that day I commenced a tape recorded interview with DOE.

Present was PC ANDERSON.

At 21:45 that day the interview was concluded. The master tape was signed and sealed and I referred to it as Police item JR/1.

SCENARIOS

This section goes through different scenarios that other Police officers have attended or dealt with. The idea is to go through each scenario and ask some key questions of both good and bad practice. At any situation there is always more than one way you can handle it. The idea of the scenario is to get you thinking and assessing a situation. You need to look at the safety of the public, yourself and your colleagues to come to the best way to resolve a situation.

When going to a scene you should always be thinking of your personal safety and often using tactical communications and seeing if talking to somebody can resolve a situation, without the use of force. You may need to be thinking about what offences have been committed and if there are any witnesses or evidence, like CCTV, , or fingerprints. There is a lot to absorb and work through initially, but by observing other Police officers, asking questions and gaining experience out on the beat, it does become easier.

Scenario 1
You are on mobile patrol with another Police working a 3 until midnight shift. It is 11:30pm and you pull up at a set of traffic lights. On looking right you notice a large group of males fighting. What do you do?
Do you call it in and go back to the station as you are due off soon?

Do you go through a red traffic light and try to stop the fight?

Do you radio through, passing on details whilst waiting for the traffic lights to change and then see what you can do?

Answer - the first reaction to the incident should be to pass details over the radio to the control room. This makes the control room aware of the situation as well as other officers on patrol. Try to observe any details.

On arrival at the scene you need to assess the situation and see if you require further assistance. Can any offenders be identified? Can you calm the situation down or break up the fight without putting yourself or your colleague at direct risk? If you can, try to break the fight up or talk to the group to quell things. Try to identify what has happened. If possible, find out if there are any injuries or any complaints being made. If there are not any then the offence in this situation is likely to be affray. Further offences may come to light once further investigation has taken place.

As the first officer on the scene you will need to convey as much information as possible, and if the situation becomes difficult then request further assistance, as two Police officers are likely to struggle with a large group of people into drink and fighting. Once further officers are on the scene you can then think about making arrests. Once offenders or persons involved in the incident have been arrested then consider if there is any CCTV in the area that can help identify offenders and what has happened.

Scenario 2

You are on foot patrol with a Special Constable, walking through a park and in the distance you see two males with cans and one of them is smoking. As the males get closer you notice that they have cans of opened beer and one male smells heavily of cannabis. The male with cannabis is searched and after the search produces a nub and asks if he can throw it away.

Do you do a stop search and walk on?

Do you do the search, confiscate the cans and walk off?

Do you confiscate the cans and charge the male smelling of drugs with possession?

Answer - the park in which males are drinking does not allow the consumption of alcohol at any time, even if the males are over 18 years of age, so the beer can be confiscated and poured away, as it is opened. By consuming alcohol they are breaking a local by law and can be fined if deemed appropriate to the situation, or given a warning.

The male who has been searched and produced the nub from smoking cannabis, is in possession of cannabis even though he is over the age of 18. He has not been given a cannabis warning before but even cannabis dust is in possession so he can be charged with possession of cannabis. As this is the first time he has been caught he can be given a cannabis warning, but on the second occasion it would be a fixed penalty notice and on the third an arrest.

Scenario 3

You and your partner are first on the scene to a serious assault. A man has been hit and pushed to the ground, causing a serious head injury and he is bleeding. The offenders are no longer at the location.

Do you go and search the area for the offenders?

Do you speak to the IP and any witnesses?

Do you speak to the IP and take details of any witnesses and cordon off the crime scene?

Answer - as the offenders have left the scene you cannot look for them without a description. You also need to take care of the victim and preserve the crime scene as a first priority.

Try to get an account of what has happened and a description of the offenders. The description can then be passed on to other Police officers in the area. Your partner can be looking to secure the area and talking to witnesses. With serious bleeding the offence is GBH. As well as taking witness details, the scene can be searched for evidence. Once treated, the IP will need photographs of the injuries for any further action or proceedings that may follow.

Scenario 4

You have been called to a local takeaway that has been repeatedly suffering racial attacks which consist of graffiti and racial verbal abuse. The group involved is again shouting abuse outside the takeaway and the owner has called the Police asking for assistance. On arrival the group is still there, but with no shouting taking place. On talking to the group they say they have not shouted or said anything, but a member of the public approaches you to inform you that they were shouting racial abuse.

Do you give them a warning and send them on their way?

As it is a repeated incident is further action needed?

Do you investigate the incident further?

Answer - as a member of the public has approached you and said there was racist abuse, it is classed as a racist incident which will need further investigation. You can consider an arrest for using threatening, abusive or insulting words or behaviour, which was racially aggravated. You can take details of individuals in the group, checking them over the radio to see if they are out on bail or have conditions of bail relating to other incidents. Then get witness statements from both the takeaway owner and members of the public to identify the key offenders within the group. Next go and arrest the offenders. Look at previous incidents to see what happened and which officer was dealing with them so that nothing is missed and the appropriate action is taken.

The group does need to be removed from the area either by arrest or by asking to leave the area.

Scenario 5

You and your partner are called to an RTC between two cars. On arrival a paramedic is on the scene. One car is jutting out of a junction and one car is at the side of a busy main road. There are minor injuries but the cars are unmovable.

Do you check the drivers are ok and leave if they are?

Do you take any details?

Do you take details and make the scene safe?

Answer - once on scene the priority is life preservation and safety of those involved. On arrival you can use your blue lights whilst stationary to warn other road users. Then control the traffic either through hand signals or by closing the road. This is a first priority. Then make sure high visibility vests are worn and the scene is safe for those involved. Your partner can assist the paramedic and then take the details from the drivers if possible. Check if there are any witnesses. If possible, an RTC requires a breath sample to be taken from both drivers to ensure the collision is not drink related. Once details have been taken and casualties attended to, recovery of the vehicles is the next priority, especially as they are causing an obstruction and cannot be moved because of damage. All forces have a recovery firm they use or the drivers can arrange their own recovery. If the vehicles are causing an obstruction then, for safety reasons, you will need to stay at the scene until they are recovered.

CAREER DEVELOPMENT

After a few years of service you may decide that you want to change what you do within the Police service. The options are wide and varied even for Special Constables

A Special Constable may decide to do extra training to specialise in an area or even work with CID. Some Specials aspire to become Special Sergeants or Inspectors which usually means attending a selection board. More recently special management are attending a weekend management course

For full-time officer who want to progress within the management structure then you have to pass your OSPRE® exams

OSPRE

The Objective Structured Performance-Related Examination (OSPRE®) was introduced nationally in 1991, as the primary means through which Police officers in England and Wales are selected for promotion to the ranks of sergeant and Inspector. It is designed to test knowledge and understanding of the law and procedure of the future sergeants and inspectors.

The examination involves 150 multiple-choice questions over a three-hour period. Questions used in the examination are prepared by trained writers who have extensive policing experience and knowledge of the relevant legislation. During the development period, all questions are extensively quality assured by a team of internal and independent experts.

Rules for OSPRE®

Admission to the qualifying examination for promotion to the rank of

Sergeant is currently restricted to regular constables (those appointed to office of regular Constable) who, by 30 November of the calendar year in which they take the OSPRE®

Part I, will have: completed not less than two years' service; and been confirmed in their appointment; and not previously obtained a pass to the rank of sergeant in a recognised Police promotion process.

Admission to the qualifying examination for promotion to the rank of Inspector is currently restricted to sergeants who, on 01 July of the calendar year in which they take the OSPRE®

Part I, will have: attained the substantive rank of sergeant 1; and not previously obtained a pass to the rank of Inspector in a recognised Police promotion process.

High Potential Development Scheme: An officer who is a member of the national High Potential Development Scheme (HPDS) may undertake OSPRE®

Part I before completing the above admission requirements. HPDS officers are subject to specific provisions made by the Police (Promotion) (Amendment) Regulations.

Structure

The Sergeants' and Inspectors' OSPRE® each consist of one process in two separate parts.

PART I The Sergeants' and Inspectors' OSPRE®

Part I consists of a single, 150 question multiple-choice paper of three hours duration.

PART II The Sergeants' and Inspectors' OSPRE®

Part II consists of a series of practical work sample exercises that constitute an assessment centre. These exercises last approximately ninety minutes and are relevant to the target rank.

Pass/Fail criteria

Part I The pass requirement in the Sergeants' and Inspectors' OSPRE®

Part I is an absolute standard (set pass mark). Those candidates who achieve a score equal to or above the set pass mark will be awarded a pass.

Further details in relation to the pass mark and the 'low band fail' and 'exceptional' cut scores will be communicated in the Instructions to Candidates document, which candidates receive prior to the examination.

Details of candidates attaining the 'exceptional' and 'low band fail' scores will be notified to their Chief Officer.

Part II

The pass requirement in the Sergeants' and Inspectors' OSPRE®

Part II is an absolute standard (set pass mark). Those candidates who achieve a score equal to or above the set pass mark will be awarded a pass.

Further details in relation to the pass mark and the 'exceptional' cut score will be communicated in the Notes for Guidance Document, which candidates receive prior to the examination.

Candidates attaining the 'exceptional' score will be notified to the Chief Officer of the candidates who attain them.

Candidates must demonstrate an acceptable level of performance in the area of Respect for Race and Diversity. Candidates' conduct during the OSPRE®

Part II should be guided by the principles in the Standards of Professional Behaviour in Schedule 1 of the Police (Conduct) Regulations 2008

Candidates who receive a D grade in Respect for Race and Diversity will be reported to the PPEB Debrief Panel. The PPEB Debrief Panel will decide on the appropriate course of action as follows:

1. no further action

2. recommend feedback to the candidate

3. recommend feedback to the candidate's Chief Officer

4. recommend that the candidate fails the overall OSPRE®

Part II.

Candidates will be informed of the PPEB Debrief Panel's decision within seven working days of the decision being made. Candidates who are subject to option four above may submit a report for consideration by the PPEB Reports & Disqualifications Panel. The report must be submitted by the candidate, and received by NPIA, within seven days of the date of the letter in which the candidate is notified of the PPEB Debrief Panel's decision. The report must be countersigned by the candidate's line manager or above.

Part II re-sit

A candidate who is unsuccessful at their first attempt at Part II may make two further attempts within five years of passing Part I.

Failure to attain the absolute standard on these occasions will mean that the candidate must re-qualify in the OSPRE®

Part I before making any further attempt at Part II.

Candidates are allowed a maximum of three attempts at Part II which must be made within five years of passing Part I (except under the Maternity Policy and Pregnant Officer Policy). Exceptions to this rule may be allowed by the Police Promotion Examinations Board on an individual basis.

Example Questions

Crime

John has had a falling out with a business colleague over their business deals. His partner has refused to sell his share of the business. Knowing that on the death of his partner he would have full control he arranges a contract killing. Unknown to John, the person he speaks to is an undercover Police officer. What is the most appropriate offence committed by John?

Answer The offence 'Solicitation of murder' is against The Offences Against the Person Act 1861:Section 4 "Whosoever shall solicit, encourage, persuade or endeavour to persuade or shall propose to any person to murder any other person, whether he be a subject of Her Majesty or not. Shall be guilty". Triable Either way Offence (Indictment only - life imprisonment)

Brian knows his neighbor is away and so, in a cunning plan, decides to make use of his absence to power his concrete mixer and other tools while Brian builds a patio in his own garden. Brian uses a coat hanger to pull the latch on the back door and open it. Inside he plugs in five extension cables running them into his back garden. Brian uses the cables to power a number of tools whilst he works. With regard to Brian's actions, which of the following statements is true?

Answer Under 9(1)(a) and (b) "stealing" means "an intention to commit theft". However, this does not include abstracting electricity. The property which is intended to be stolen must be in the building or part of a building (Low v Blease (1975)).

Evidence and Procedure

Sergeant Fisher the custody officer is considering bail conditions for Godfrey who is presently in custody for an offence. Which is NOT a condition that a custody officer can impose?

Answer A custody officer may only refuse to grant bail on the grounds of further offences if that offence relates to an imprisonable offence not any offence. In making the decision the custody officer should consider if the person has committed offences whilst previously on bail.

Section 16 of the Crime and Disorder Act 1998 deals with the removal of truants and in the section makes reference to a designated premises. What is a designated place?

Answer Although a designated place is not defined in the act however they are a matter for the local authority.

General Police Duties

An Anti-Social Behaviour Order is an order to prevent an individual acting in an anti-social manner. Which does form part of the definition of anti-social?

Answer Anti-Social Behaviour is defined as a manner that caused or was likely to cause harassment, alarm or distress to one or more persons and not of the same house hold as himself.

In order to apply for an Anti-Social Behaviour Order, it must appear to the relevant authority that a person acted in a manner that caused or was likely to cause, harassment, alarm or distress. Who, or what is the relevant authority that can apply for such an order?

Answer The relevant authority is BOTH the Local Authority and the Chief Officer of Police, any part of whose area lies within the area of the local authority. Housing action trusts and social landlords are also included.

Road Policing

Section 148(1) of the Road Traffic Act 1988 (requirements for insurance) makes the effects of some restrictions in a policy void. If a policy purports to restrict the extent of its cover by reference to certain features, breaches of them by the insured person will not affect the validity of that policy for the purpose of section 143. Which if any of the following would NOT be covered by this section?

Answer The list covered by S.148 is far reaching, previous driving convictions however is not included.

With regard to the penalty for causing death by dangerous driving, which of the following statements are true?

Answer Causing Death by Dangerous Driving carries an obligatory 2 year minimum disqualification and a compulsory re-test. It is an indictable offence. The re-test and disqualification applies regardless of what sentence the defendant receives.

NPIA

The NPIA is a policing organisation acting as a central resource to the Police service, working for ACPO (Association of Chief Police Officers), APA (Association of Police Authorities) and the Home Office to improve the delivery of policing. Alongside driving improvements in the Police service, it is responsible for managing critical national infrastructure and developing wider links to support the adoption of proven ideas from outside sources. In the current economic climate there main focus is on efficiencies and reducing costs especially for IT procurement as an example. Others include looking at more collaboration as a way to reduce cost and improve efficiency.

The NPIA has the following the remit to improve public safety through the provision of:

•Providing critical national services

•Building capability across the police service

•Providing professional expertise to police forces and authorities

For 2011-2013 they have the following business plan:

Improved Cost Effectiveness

1. Implement £19 million of national police non-IT procurement savings.

2. Reduce the volume of doctrine, guidance and standards by 20per cent and develop and improve the commissioning process.

3. Reduce the overall number of core Manual of Guidance forms by 15 per cent and to develop and agree national guidance to drive the delivery of proportionate case file content in relation to each case

4. Deliver with the service £100 million worth of efficiency savings using Quest and other business improvement models.

Improve Public Confidence in Policing

5. Equip a further 10,000 front-line officers with mobile devices such as BlackBerry's, enhancing the capabilities to support officers in confirming identities in real time, enabling forces to deliver efficiency savings.

6. Complete pilots in three forces of the accelerated DNA identification/elimination systems, which will enable forces to procure the technology in 2012.

7. Support forces and the tripartite in the delivery of the Safe and Confident Neighbourhoods Strategy.

8. Undertake a national Neighbourhood Policing stock take to include identification of good practice and areas for improvement.

9. Identify emerging effective practice and develop a Tactical Diagnostic Toolkit to support the police and their partners in responding to local crime and anti-social behaviour problems.

10. Provide bespoke support to embed, sustain and develop local policing in response to the needs of police forces.

Strengthen Protective Services

11. Deliver those activities in the current (baselined) Schengen Information System (SIS) Programme Schedule that fall within the financial year 2010/11 and to demonstrate robust financial control of SIS Programme and its component projects.

12. Deliver Olympics Airwave infrastructure.

13. Develop and deliver agreed products for the Communications Capabilities Directorate.

14. Deliver £10 million worth of cashable savings through the delivery and further development of the collaboration support centre.

15. Provide specific support to police forces and police authorities to ensure they meet the ACPO (2008) Minimum Standards.

Improved Leadership and workforce capability

16. Demonstrate through working with candidates and police authorities a reported improvement in readiness and quality of ACPO candidates in preparation to deliver subsequent appropriate improvements.

17. Assess all learning programmes and, where relevant, ensure that business and financial management skills are fully integrated.

18. Deliver a package of specified HR, Workforce and Learning Practices and Process, mapped to the 'Police Productivity Framework', which will allow forces to report improved efficiencies in 2011/12.

19. Provide peer support to forces and authorities in using the 'Police Productivity Framework' to achieve positive outcomes.

Improved Management and use of information by frontline ISIS

20. Deliver the new Police National Database as part of the IMPACT change programme to enable effective sharing of information within the policing community, and realising the final tranche of £1.5 million in cashable savings per annum.

21. Enable forces to deliver the Information Systems Improvement Strategy (ISIS) efficiency savings of £25 million, through rationalising and converging applications and infrastructure.

22. Provide peer support to selected forces and authorities to implement ISIS based systems.

INDEX

2930245R00115

Printed in Great Britain
by Amazon.co.uk, Ltd.,
Marston Gate.